LIVING IN THE PRESENCE OF GOD

The Works and Life of Brother Lawrence
with Devotions by Steve Troxel

I1027901

Living in The Presence of God

The Works and Life of Brother Lawrence
With Devotions by Steve Troxel

Published By

God's Daily Word Ministries
PO Box 700113
San Antonio, TX 78270

Copyright © 2002 by God's Daily Word Ministries.
ISBN 0-9708531-3-0

Cover Design by Al Mendenhall
Creative Vision Studio, San Antonio, Texas

Printed in Canada

Edited by Steve Troxel

All Scripture quotations, unless otherwise indicated, are taken from the
Holy Bible, New International Version®. NIV®. Copyright ©1973, 1978,
1984 by International Bible Society. Used by permission of Zondervan
Publishing House. All rights reserved.

CONTENTS

PREFACE

Brother Lawrence was born Nicholas Herman in France in the early 1600's. He became a monk in 1649 and remained in the same Paris monastery until his death in 1691. During his time in the monastery, he became known for his simple and practical faith. The last forty years of his life were lived in one continual conversation with God, which he maintained whether in formal prayer or in the busyness of the kitchen where he worked.

The first four parts of this book were all originally written in the late 1600's. The Letters and Principles were written by Brother Lawrence himself, and the Conversations and Character sections were written by Joseph de Beaufort. Beaufort met with Brother Lawrence on several occasions and was responsible for getting his thoughts into print and initially distributing them to as many people as possible. I have edited each section to flow with today's English while prayerfully maintaining the thoughts of the original work. The devotions in part five of this book were written to continue the theme of the presence of God.

Jesus said the greatest of all commandments is: "Love the Lord your God with all your heart and with all your soul and with all your mind and with all your strength," (Mark 12:30). Brother Lawrence gives us a glimpse of what it means to carry out this command in our daily lives. Granted, the presence of God may be easier to find in a monastery than in our present environment with all our pressures and near insane busyness, but we must not miss the message; there is a place of peace and contentment where we are being called today! Even in the midst of our thousands of distractions, we can learn the discipline of living in the presence of God.

Steve Troxel

5

PART ONE

CONVERSATIONS WITH

BROTHER LAWRENCE

BY

JOSEPH DE BEAUFORT

CONVERSATIONS WITH BROTHER LAWRENCE

FIRST CONVERSATION
THE THIRD OF AUGUST, 1666

The first time I saw Brother Lawrence he told me that God had given him a single blessing in his conversion at the age of eighteen.

One day in winter, seeing a tree stripped of its leaves, and considering that in a little while the leaves would be renewed, and after that the flowers and fruit would appear, he received an exceptionally high view of the providence and power of God. Since that time, this view has never been removed from his soul. It had perfectly set him free from the world and gave him such an instant love for God, that he could not tell whether it had increased in the past forty years.

He said he had been a footman to Mr. Fieubert, the treasurer, and was an awkward fellow who broke everything. He had desired to enter a monastery, thinking he would be disciplined there for his awkwardness and faults, and in this way would sacrifice his life, with all its pleasures, to God - but God had disappointed him, because in the monastery he found nothing but joy and satisfaction.

He said we should firmly establish ourselves in the presence of God by continually conversing with Him; and that it was a shameful thing to quit our divine conversation to think of trivial and foolish thoughts. We should feed and nourish our souls with high notions of God, which produce a great joy in being devoted to Him.

He said we should make our faith come alive and that it was very sad we had so little. Instead of allowing our life to be completely ruled by faith, we amuse ourselves with trivial acts of devotion which change daily. Living fully by faith is the spirit of the Church, and is sufficient to bring us into the perfect presence of God.

He said we ought to give ourselves to God in pure abandonment, with regard both to things temporal and Spiritual. We should seek our satisfaction only in doing His will, whether He leads us by suffering or by blessings, for all would be equal to a soul truly resigned. We must be faithful in those times of dryness, by which God tries our love for Him; for then is the time to draw closer and more effectively resign ourselves to Him. Such an attitude during a single dry season could promote much Spiritual advancement.

As for the miseries and sins he heard of daily in the world, he said he was never astonished about them; on the contrary, he was surprised there were not more, considering the wickedness of which sinners were capable. He earnestly prayed for them; but knowing that God, in His timing, would apply the remedy for their wrongs, he gave it no further thought.

He said that to arrive at such resignation as God desires, we should carefully watch over all the passions which interfere with Spiritual concerns as well as with those which can cause great physical and emotional harm. God would reveal those passions to those who truly desire to serve Him. He said if my purpose was to sincerely serve God, I could come to him (Brother Lawrence) as often as I pleased, without any fear of being troublesome; but if not, that I should not visit him again.

SECOND CONVERSATION
THE TWENTY-EIGHTH OF SEPTEMBER, 1666

He said he was completely governed by love, with no other interest; not even whether he would be lost or saved. But having resolved to make the love of God the end of all his actions, he had found reasons enough to be satisfied. He was sufficiently pleased when he could take up a straw from the ground for the love of God, seeking only Him and nothing else, not even His gifts - only Him.

This attitude of his soul resulted in endless gifts of grace from God; but often in receiving the fruit of those blessings, he found it necessary to reject their sweet pleasure. He said that the gift was not God Himself, since he knew by faith that God was infinitely greater; it was far better to continue going to God beyond His gift. God would repay so readily and liberally for everything one did for Him, that at times he wished he could hide from God what he did, so that by receiving no reward, he might have the joy of doing something purely for the love of God and God alone.

He said that for a period of four years he had been in great anguish from a certain belief that he was lost, and that all the men in the world could not have persuaded him otherwise. During this time he suffered much; but he had reasoned with himself, saying: "I engaged in this religious life only for the love of God, and I have sought to act only for Him; whatever becomes of me, whether lost or saved, I will always continue to live purely for the love of God. I will at least hold onto this: knowing that till death I shall have done all that is in me to love Him." Since then he had not worried about Heaven or Hell; all his life had been lived in perfect freedom and continual joy. He said he placed his sins between him and God, as though to tell Him he did not deserve His blessings, but that God still continued to give them in abundance. At times, he felt that God would lead him by the hand before all the heavenly court to display the wretch to whom He took pleasure in granting His grace.

In order to form a habit of continually conversing with God and seeking His counsel in all we do, he said, at first, we must seek Him and draw near with some diligence and perseverance; but after a short while we would find an inward excitement stirred by His love and would be drawn to Him without any difficulty.

He expected that after the pleasant days God had given him, he should have his turn of pain and suffering; but he was not uneasy about it, knowing very well, that since he could do nothing of himself, God would not fail to give him the necessary strength. When he set himself to the task of putting some virtue into practice, he would address God, saying; "Lord, I cannot do this unless You enable me." He would then immediately be given the grace to proceed.

He said that when he fell short in his duty, he would simply confess his fault to God, saying; "I can never do anything but fail, if You leave me to myself. It is You who must prevent me from falling, and mend what is not right." After this, he gave himself no further concern over his fault; and when he succeeded in his duty, he gave God thanks, acknowledging that all success came from Him.

He said we ought to act very simply with God, speaking to Him frankly and plainly, and asking for His help in all our situations as soon as they happen. His experience was that God would never fail to perfectly respond.

He had recently been sent into Burgundy, to buy the provision of wine for the society. This was a very unwelcome task for him because he had no aptitude for business, was lame in one leg, and could only go about the boat by rolling himself over the casks. However, he was not concerned about this, nor about the purchase of the wine. He told God it was His business he was about, and afterward found everything worked out very well.

Likewise, while working in the kitchen, a job which he naturally disliked, he trained himself to do everything there for the love of God. With continual prayer for His grace to do his work well, he found everything easy during the fifteen years he had been employed there. He was now in the cobbler's workshop and was very happy; but he was always ready to leave his job, since his greatest pleasure came from simply doing little things for the love of God.

He said the set times of prayer were in no way different for him than any other. He would retire to pray at the times directed by his Superiors, but he did not want such retirement, nor ask for it, because his most demanding work did not divert him from the presence of God.

Knowing he must love God in all things, he sought to do so and felt he had no need of a director to give him advice; but he certainly felt the need for someone to hear his confessions. He was very much aware of his faults, but not discouraged by them. He would confess them to God, without making any excuse, and afterward, would peacefully resume his usual practice of worship and love.

In his troubles, he had not consulted anyone, but knowing only by faith that God was present, he was content with directing all his actions to Him; doing them with a desire to please Him, and accepting whatever would come of it. He said that useless thoughts spoil the presence of God and are the beginning of all evil. We should reject them, as soon as they are perceived as unnecessary to the matter at hand or for our Spiritual growth, and return immediately to our communion with God. In the beginning he had often spent his entire time appointed for prayer in rejecting wandering thoughts and falling into them again. At first he used spoken prayers, but this habit had eventually passed and now he never ordered his time of prayer by a set of rules.

He said he was not strong enough to ask God for repentant acts to discipline him for his sin, nor did he want them, but he knew he truly deserved them. He also knew that if God should send them, He would also give him the grace to endure. He had found that all such acts of repentance and all other formal exercises only serve to advance the union with God through love; and after he had deeply pondered this, he found it was quicker to go straight to God by a continual exercise of love, and doing ALL things for His sake. We should make a great distinction between the acts we do based on our understanding, or perception of a need, and those which flow from our desire to love; since, in the end, our understanding counted very little. Our only business was to love and delight ourselves in God.

He said that all of our good effort and deeds, could not remove a single sin. Without concern, we should expect the pardon of our sins by the Blood of Jesus Christ and only strive to love Him with all our heart. He found that God seemed to grant the greatest blessings to the greatest sinners, as the best way of displaying His mercy.

He had determined that the greatest pains or pleasures of this world could not compare with the pain and pleasure he had experienced in his spirit: so he was concerned about nothing, feared nothing, and asked for nothing, desiring only that he might not offend God. He felt he was not capable of doing great things for God, so he was content to simply do small things for the love of God. With that done, he knew nothing would happen to him except what God should will, and of that he had no concern.

THIRD CONVERSATION
THE TWENTY-SECOND OF NOVEMBER, 1666

He told me, that his foundation of the Spiritual life had been a high notion and esteem of God held in place by faith. When he had fully grasped this, he had no other care than to faithfully reject every other thought so he might perform all his actions for the love of God. When he would sometimes go a long while without thinking of God, he did not trouble himself about it; but after having confessed to God, he returned to Him with all the more greater trust in Him, having a deeper sense of his wretchedness in having wandered away. The trust we place in God honors Him much, and causes us to receive many blessings. He said it was impossible, not only for God to deceive us, but also that He would allow our soul to suffer for very long when it was perfectly resigned to Him; he therefore resolved to endure everything for His sake.

He had often experienced God's ready and prompt grace with all sorts of mental diversions and temptations. Thus, when he had mundane business to do, he did not concern himself with it in advance; but when it was time to do it, he found in God, as in a clear mirror, all that was necessary.

When his work even slightly diverted him from the thought of God, a fresh reminder would capture his soul. This would give him a stronger sense of God, and so inflame and transport his soul, that at times it was difficult to contain himself; in fact, he was more united to God in his common activities than when he engaged in the more formal acts of devotion. He would often return from these times with much dryness in his soul.

He expected there would come a time of great pain in his body or mind; but that the worst that could happen to him was to lose the sense of God, which he had enjoyed so long. But the goodness of God assured him he would not be completely abandoned, and that God would give him strength to bear whatever evil He permitted. Therefore, he feared nothing, and had no need to consult with anybody about his condition. When he had attempted to do so, he had always come away with less understanding than when he sought counsel. He was willing to readily lay down his life for the love of God, so he had no apprehension of danger. He said this perfect resignation to God was the only sure way to know which path to follow.

He said that in the beginning of the Spiritual life - the life where we live in the presence of God - we ought to faithfully accomplish our duties and deny ourselves; but that after a short time, there were only unspeakable pleasures. In difficulties we need only turn to Jesus Christ, and ask for His grace, after which everything becomes easy.

The reason many Christian do not grow, is because they become entangled in doing specific good deeds and particular acts of devotion, while they neglect the love of God which is the desired end result. This is obvious to see by their works, and is the reason we see so little Godly character. There is no special skill or knowledge required for going to God, only a heart completely determined to apply itself only to Him, to live for Him, and to love Him only.

FOURTH CONVERSATION
THE TWENTY-FIFTH OF NOVEMBER, 1667

He spoke with me often, and with great openness from his heart regarding his way of going to God. He told me that it consisted of, once and for all, turning away and rejecting everything which we know does not lead to God, in order that we might develop the habit of continual conversation with Him - conversation which is simple and without anything artificial. We only need to recognize that God is intimately present with us; He is always by our side, ready to answer our prayers for knowing His will when there is doubt, and ready to provide strength to properly accomplish what we clearly see. We should offer everything to Him before we begin, and thank Him when we are done. In this continual conversation with God, we should be preoccupied with praising, worshiping, and always loving Him for His infinite goodness and perfection.

He said that without being discouraged about our sins, we should pray and ask for His grace with a perfect confidence, while relying on His promise to forgive. God never fails to offer His grace at every turn; he had a good understanding of this and only failed to ask for His help when he wandered from God's presence.

If our only desire is to please and love God, He will always give us light in our times of doubt. Our growing closer to God does not depend on changing what we do, but in doing our common tasks for the love of God. He said it was sad to see how many people mistook the means for the end, placing all their effort in the performance of certain works, which were poorly accomplished anyway because of their selfish concerns. He had found the best way to draw near to God was to do everything, without concern for pleasing others, purely for the love of God, and to do so to the very best of his ability.

He said it was a delusion to think the times of prayer were, or ought to be, different from other times. We are as equally obligated to stay close to God in our busy times of action, as in our specified quiet times of prayer. His prayer was nothing but a deep sense of the presence of God, his soul unaware of all else but love for God: and when the appointed time of prayer was over, he found no difference, because he continued in the presence of God, praising and blessing Him with all his might. Thus, he passed his life in continual joy; yet, he actually hoped that God would give him some difficulties in his life so he could grow stronger.

We ought to, once and for all, put our complete trust in God, and make a total surrender of ourselves to Him, knowing that He would never deceive us. We should not grow weary of doing little things for the love of God; He does not regard the greatness of the work, but the love with which it is performed. In the beginning, we should not be surprised nor upset if we fail to draw near to God; but if we persist, we will naturally come into His presence, with little effort or thought, and yield a life of wondrous joy.

He said the whole substance of our relationship with God was faith, hope, and love; the practice and nourishment of which would utterly unite us to His will. All besides these were unimportant and should be used as a means to absorb us in the final goal of love. All things are possible for him who believes, less difficult for him who hopes, more easy for him who loves, and still easier for him who perseveres in the practice of all three virtues. Our life's goal should be to become the most perfect worshippers of God we can possibly be - the worshipers we hope to be through all eternity.

When we determine to live the Spiritual life, we should consider, and examine to the very depths of our heart, who we really are. When we do, we will find ourselves to be worthy of all contempt and not deserving the name of Christian. We deserve to be subject to all kinds of misery and a great multitude of troubles. After this, we should not wonder that trials, temptations, and oppositions of all kinds happen to us.

On the contrary, we should submit to them and bear them for as long as God desires, knowing that such experiences are used to advance our Spiritual growth. We should learn to praise Him through the trials and then continue to praise Him when the trials have passed. The closer we approach to God's presence and holiness, the more we realize our complete dependence on God's grace.

Since Brother Lawrence had found such an advantage in walking in the presence of God, it was natural for him to earnestly recommend it to others; but his example was a stronger witness than any argument he could propose. His very countenance was edifying; he had such a sweet and calm devotion that he could not help but influence those who observed him.

PART TWO

THE LETTERS OF

BROTHER LAWRENCE

THE LETTERS OF BROTHER LAWRENCE

FIRST LETTER
THE FIRST OF JUNE, 1682

Press on to a fuller practice of the presence of God.

I am writing to you regarding the thoughts of one of our society (he is referring to himself), about the continual blessings he receives from the presence of God. May we both benefit from them.

This brother has been careful to remain in the presence of God for more than the past thirty years; and to do, say, or think nothing which would displease Him. He does everything with no other concern than the love of God because he realizes that God deserves infinitely more.

He is now so accustomed to the presence of God that he receives continual help from Him on all occasions. For the past thirty years, his soul has been filled with such constant and elevated joys, that he is sometimes forced to moderate them to keep them from bursting forth in childish expressions.

If he sometimes wanders from that Divine presence, God causes Himself to be felt so intimately in his soul that he quickly returns. This often happens when he is engaged in his daily work, but he obediently responds to God's appeal by a lifting of his heart to God, or through a sweet and loving thought, or by whatever words as his love may form - words such as; "My God, here I am all devoted to You. Lord, make me according to Your heart." And then it seems that God, satisfied with such few words, returns to rest in the depth and center of his soul. These experiences give him such an assurance that God is always near, that he is incapable of doubting it in any situation.

Judge from this what contentment and satisfaction he enjoys: while he continually finds such a great treasure, he no longer anxiously searches for it; but having it open before him, he is free to take what ever he desires.

He often talks about our blindness and is filled with sorrow that we are satisfied with so little of God. He says that God has infinite blessings to give and we stop with trivial and momentary devotions. In our blindness, we hinder the hand of God and restrict the flow of His grace. But when God finds a soul filled with a live and active faith, He pours out His blessings of grace in such an abundance, they cannot be stopped.

Yes, we often stop the flow of His blessings by the little value we place on them. But let us stop them no more; let us examine our heart and break down any barriers which keep us from His presence. Let us redeem the lost time and make a clear path for His blessings. We only have a little remaining time, for death is not far away. Let us be well prepared; for we only die once, and then we must give an account for every thought, word, and deed.

There is no more room for delay. I commend you for the essential steps you have already taken, but we must continue to press on, because not to move ahead in the Spiritual life is to move backward. Those who have the mind of the Holy Spirit move forward even while they sleep. If the small ship of our soul becomes tossed with the wind and storms, let us awaken the Lord, and He will quickly calm the sea.

I have taken the liberty to write you these thoughts so you can compare them with your own. May they serve to fan the flames of our soul. Let us both recall the intense love we had at first and benefit from the example and thoughts of this Brother. He is not well known in the world, but he is dearly loved by God. I will continue to pray for you, please urgently pray for me. I am yours in our Lord.

SECOND LETTER

Act always on the principle of love.

I received two books and a letter from a Sister who is preparing to make her vows. She asked that you and your society pray for her; I hope you will not disappoint her. Plead with God for her to make her sacrifice based only on love for Him and with a firm resolve to be wholly devoted to Him.

I will send you one of the books which deals with the practice of the presence of God. In my opinion, this practice is everything needed for a complete Spiritual life; for being Spiritual means to abide in His presence. A continual and proper abiding requires the heart to be empty of all other things. Only then can God take full possession and do in us what He pleases.

There is nothing in this world more sweet and delightful than a continual conversation with God. Only those who have practiced and experienced His presence can understand; yet I do not want you to seek His presence for that motive. It is not pleasure we should seek, but simply His presence because we love Him; and because He has invited us to come.

If I were a preacher, I would preach about the practice of the presence of God more than any other subject; and if I were a director, I would recommend it to the entire world. This is how necessary I believe it to be - and so easy to follow.

If we only understood the amount of grace we need from God, we would never lose sight of Him - not even for a moment. Please believe me and make an immediate and firm resolution never to willfully forget Him. Resolve to spend the rest of your days in His sacred presence - in whatever circumstances He desires - because you love Him with ALL your heart. If you are disciplined and continue with this practice, you will soon see results and be blessed.

THIRD LETTER
THE THIRD OF NOVEMBER, 1685

Encouragement to persevere.

I received from Mrs. N the things which you gave her for me. I am wondering why you did not write me your thoughts about the book I sent you dealing with the practice of the presence of God. I encourage you to set your heart toward this practice in your old age - it is better late than never.

I cannot imagine how people who desire to serve the Lord can live a satisfied life without practicing the presence of God. I keep myself with Him in the very center of my soul as much as I can, and while I am with Him, I fear nothing; but the smallest turning away causes me great anguish.

This exercise does not tire the body. However, it is proper to sometimes deprive the body of little pleasures, even though they are innocent and lawful: for God will not permit a soul, which desires to be entirely devoted to Him, to be consumed with pleasures besides Him - this is more than reasonable. I am not saying we must place strict constraints on ourselves. No, we must serve God with a holy freedom; we must faithfully serve, without distress or anxiety, bringing our mind gently back to God each time we find it has wandered from Him.

It's necessary that we place our complete trust in God. We must lay aside all other cares, even some special forms of devotion. Though these may be good in themselves, they have the ability to entangle us and actually keep us distant from God. The purpose of any devotional act is to bring us to God; so when we learn to live each moment in His presence, it becomes useless to return to the specific acts. Rather, we may continue our communion of love while abiding in His holy presence through all forms of praise, worship, thanksgiving, longing, surrender, or any other form our spirit can invent.

Do not be discouraged by the inner distaste you may find when you initially attempt this exercise; you must be disciplined. At first, many think it is a waste of time; but you must continue and resolve to persevere until death even though there may be difficulties. I commend myself to the prayers of you and your holy society. I am yours in our Lord.

FOURTH LETTER

To live and die with God.

I feel truly sorry for you. It is best if you can leave the management of your affairs to others and spend the rest of your life worshipping God. He does not ask us for much; a brief moment of remembrance, a little love: sometimes a prayer for His grace or to lift up our troubles, and sometimes to thank Him for our many blessings. He continues to bless us even in the midst of our troubles; we should therefore comfort ourselves in Him as often as we can. Any time is the proper time to lift your heart to Him; and even the smallest remembrance is always acceptable to Him. You don't need to cry out very loud; for He is nearer than we think.

It is not necessary to be at church to be with God; we can make a sanctuary in our heart and converse with Him in meekness, humility and love. Everyone is capable of intimate conversation with God, some more than others - He knows each of our capabilities. Let's resolve to begin today! Perhaps He is waiting for us to make a genuine commitment - have courage!

You are nearly sixty-four and I am almost eighty. Let's live and die with God. Our sufferings will be sweet and pleasant while we are with Him; and our greatest pleasures, if experienced without Him, will be as a cruel punishment. May He be blessed in ALL!

Develop the habit, even little by little, of worshiping Him, requesting His grace, and offering Him your heart. Do not become restricted by a certain set of rules or particular form of devotion, but live with love and humility, and a general confidence in God. You may be assured of my prayers as I am your servant in the Lord.

FIFTH LETTER

How to form the habit of being in God's presence.

Since you earnestly desire for me to share with you the method I used to arrive at the habit of being in the presence of God - the habit which He has given to me by His grace - I must tell you, it is with great difficulty that I yield to your request. I do it only on the condition that you show my letter to no one. If I knew that you would show my letter to others, I would not write to you - no matter how much I desired for you to grow. The account I can give you is this:

Having found in many books different methods of going to God, and different practices of the Spiritual life, I determined they would confuse rather than lead me to the goal of being completely God's. This made me resolve to give my all for The ALL. For the love of God, I renounced everything that was not Him; giving myself wholly to God to show my thankfulness for the forgiveness of my sins. I began to live my life as if there was no one in the world except He and I.

Sometimes I would consider myself to be as a poor criminal at the feet of Him as Judge; at other times I beheld Him in my heart as my Father and as my God. I worshipped Him as often as I could, keeping my mind in His holy presence, and recalling it as often as I found it wandering from Him. In the beginning this was a painful exercise; and yet, even with all the difficulties, I continued without being troubled or anxious when my mind had involuntarily wandered from Him. I made this my primary concern throughout the day - during the appointed times of prayer as well as the common events of life. Every moment of the day, even during the times of great busyness, I turned away everything that was capable of interrupting my thoughts of God.

This has been my common practice ever since I entered into a religious life. Though I have practiced it very imperfectly, I have still received many great blessings. I am very well aware that these blessings are given solely by the mercy and goodness of God, because we can do nothing without Him - and I even less than any other. But when we faithfully remain in His holy presence, and set Him always before us, we are not only restrained in willful disobedience which offends and displeases God, but we also gain a holy familiarity with our Heavenly Father. We obtain the freedom to successfully ask for the graces we so desperately need. By repeating these acts often, they will become a habit, and we will naturally enter the presence of God.

Please join me in giving thanks for His great goodness toward me - a goodness I will never fully appreciate since He has given so many blessings to such a miserable sinner. May all things praise His name. Amen.

SIXTH LETTER

Consistent and persistent faith.

I have not found my way of life written in any books, and although I am not concerned, I would feel much better if you would let me know your thoughts on this matter.

In a recent conversation with a man of strong religious character, I was told the Spiritual life was a life of grace, which begins with a submissive fear, is then increased by hope of eternal life, and is made complete by pure love; that in this process, there were different stages by which one finally arrives at that blessed union with God.

I have not followed this method for coming to God. Though I can't say why, it filled me with fear and discouragement. This is why, from the very beginning, I simply made the resolution to give myself completely to God and, for the love of Him, to renounce everything apart from Him.

In the beginning, I would usually occupy my time set aside for prayer with thoughts of death, judgement, hell, heaven, and my sin. I continued for several years to carefully apply my mind to the presence of God during the remainder of each day; even in the middle of my work I looked upon God as being always near and often within the very depths of my heart. I was eventually able to maintain this same closeness with God during my time set aside for prayer - this gave me great delight and comfort. The continual presence of God produced such a high and exalted notion of God that I was satisfied only by faith.

This is how I began; and yet I must tell you that for the first ten years I suffered much. I was filled with apprehension that I was not devoted to God as much as He wished; my past sins were always present in my mind, and His continual goodness and grace only produced guilt and sorrow. During this time, I often fell but then rose again and continued on. It seemed that man, reason, and even God were against me; and that the only thing in my favor was faith. I was sometimes troubled with the thought that it was only my presumption which believed I had received such favor from God - a favor which immediately placed me at the point where others reach only with much effort and hard work. Other times I thought I might be deceiving myself and that there was no Salvation for me at all.

When I thought my days of trouble would never end (which did not at all reduce the trust I had in God and only served to increase my faith), I was suddenly changed. My soul, which had been greatly troubled, felt a deep inner peace as if it had finally found a place of rest. Since that time, I walk simply before God, in faith, with humility and love; and I diligently apply myself to do or think nothing which may displease Him. I hope that when I have done all I can, He will do with me whatever He desires.

I cannot express what goes on in me at the present time. I am not concerned or distressed about my condition, because I have no will of my own other than that of God. I strive to do His will in all things, and I am so resigned that I do not wish to even pick up a straw from the ground against His command or by any motive other than pure love for Him.

I have quit all forms of formal devotion and prayer except those which my Superior's require. Rather, I devote myself only to abiding in His holy presence. I remain in this state by keeping my eyes on God and my heart set on loving Him - by making a habit of a silent conversation of the soul with God. This is the actual presence of God which causes me such contentment and joy that I am sometimes forced to dampen my outward, often childish, expressions and prevent their appearance to others.

I am assured beyond all doubt that my soul has been in the presence of God for the past thirty years. I have omitted many details which I don't feel would be of interest, but I believe it's important to let you know how I perceive myself as I stand in the presence of God, my Lord and King.

I consider myself to be a most wretched man, full of fault and corruption; a man who has committed all sorts of crimes against his King. I have a very real sense of regret as I confess all my wickedness to Him; and in asking His forgiveness, I abandon myself into His hand and accept whatever He pleases to do with me. This King is full of mercy and love, and rather than disciplining me, He embraces me with love, invites me to eat at His table, serves me with His own hands and gives me the key to His treasures. He takes pleasure in continually talking with me, blessing me in a thousand different ways, and treating me in all respects as His very favorite child. This is how I most often consider myself while in His holy presence.

My usual method is simply to give Him my full attention and to love Him with all my heart, soul, mind and strength. I often find myself attached to God with greater sweetness and delight than an infant at the mother's breast. If I could be so bold as to use this expression, I would choose to call this condition the bosom of God because of the inexpressible sweetness which I am allowed to taste and experience there. If, for whatever reason, I wander from His presence, I am quickly recalled by inward thoughts of God that are so charming and delicious I am ashamed to even mention them.

I would much rather you think about my sinful condition, of which you are well informed, than upon the great blessings which God has given one as unworthy and ungrateful as I.

My set hours of prayer have become a continuation of the same exercise. Sometimes while in prayer, I consider myself to be a stone in the hands of a mighty sculptor who is proceeding to make a beautiful statue. I present myself in this way to God and desire for Him to make His perfect image in my soul; and for Him not to stop until He makes me entirely like Himself.

At other times of prayer, I feel my spirit and soul lifted up without any thought or effort, and continue until suspended -

firmly fixed in the presence of God - where it finds a wonderful place of rest.

I know that some people criticize this condition as being inactive and full of self-love and delusion. I confess that it is a holy inactivity and would be a blessed self-love, if the soul in that state were capable of loving anyone or anything but God. When the soul is truly in the presence of God, all acts of the flesh, which would normally provide encouragement to continue, now become nothing but a hindrance. But I cannot bear that this should be called a delusion, because the soul which enjoys God in this manner desires nothing but Him. If this has become a delusion in me, it can only be changed by God Himself. He may do whatever He pleases within me: I desire only Him and to be wholly devoted to Him.

I hope you will send me your thoughts on this matter. I value your opinions and respect your reverence. I am yours in the Lord.

SEVENTH LETTER
THE TWELFTH OF OCTOBER, 1688

Encouragement for a soldier friend to trust in God.

We have a God who is infinitely gracious, and knows all our needs and desires. He will come in His perfect timing, and when you least expect Him. Hope in Him now more than ever. Thank Him with me for the blessings He has given you, particularly for the strength and patience He gives you in this time of great afflictions; it is plain to see He cares for you. Comfort yourself in Him and give thanks for everything.

I admire the strength and courage of Mr. N. God has given him a good disposition and a good will; but there is still a little of the world and a great deal of youth in him. I hope the trial which God has sent him will serve as a complete remedy for his soul, and cause him to look deep inside himself. This is a good opportunity to encourage him to put all his trust in God, who is with him wherever he goes. Let him think of God as often as he can, especially in the times of greatest danger. Even a small lifting of the heart to God - a moment of remembrance or a single act of worship - is acceptable and pleasing to Him. These moments of devotion may even come while holding a sword during a long march; and rather than reducing a soldier's courage in times of danger, they serve to make it stronger.

Please encourage him to develop the habit of thinking of God; this habit is perceived by no one, and nothing is easier than internally adoring God throughout the day. It is most necessary for a soldier who is exposed to daily life-threatening dangers. I hope God will assist him and all his family - I send them my greetings. I am, in all ways, theirs and yours.

EIGHTH LETTER

Concerning wandering thoughts in prayer.

You have not told me anything new - we are all troubled with wandering thoughts. Our mind is always given to extreme roving; but since the will is the master of all our faculties, it must recall the mind and carry it back to God.

When the mind has not been properly subdued in the beginning, but has developed bad habits of wandering and being unable to focus, it is difficult to control. It will often pull us, even against our will, to worldly thoughts.

I believe the cure for this is to confess our faults and humble ourselves before God. I do not advise you to use many words in prayer as these can often cause us to wander. Rather, keep yourself in prayer like a dumb and paralyzed beggar at a rich man's gate: give your full attention to remaining in the presence of the Lord. If your mind sometimes wanders and withdraws from Him, do not become troubled; this only serves to further distract the mind. The will must gently and peacefully bring our mind back to God. If you persevere in this manner, God will assist in holding your thoughts with Him.

One way to make it easier to recall the mind during our times of prayer, and to peacefully continue in prayer, is to not allow the mind to wander too far from God during the other times of the day. You should keep your mind focused on the presence of God at all times. When we become accustomed to thinking of Him often, it will be much easier to maintain calm thoughts of Him during prayer - or at least easier to return our mind when it wanders.

I have already told you of the many blessings we receive from this practice of the presence of God; let's be serious about it and pray for one another.

NINTH LETTER
THE TWENTY-EIGHTH OF MARCH, 1689

Redeem the lost time.

I am enclosing a letter to Sister N. which I pray you will deliver. She seems full of good will, but she desires to go faster than grace will allow - we cannot become holy all at once. I entrust her into your care. We should both assist her by our counsel, and even more by our good example. Please let me know about her from time to time. Let me know if she is remaining passionate and obedient to God.

We should keep in mind that our only purpose in this life is to please God by bringing Him glory and honor - all besides this is foolishness and driven by vanity. You and I have lived the religious life for more than forty years. Have we properly spent every one of these years loving and serving God? We must never forget that He has called us for this very purpose. I am filled with shame when I reflect on the many blessings which God has given me, and how He continues to give. I have made poor use of the time and have only made small Spiritual advancement.

Since by His grace we still have a few more days, let's earnestly begin to redeem the lost time and return with complete confidence to the Father of mercies who is always ready to lovingly receive us back. Let's continually think of Him and place all our trust in Him. I don't doubt we will soon see the effects of doing so; we will receive His abundant grace, with which we can do all things, and without which we can do nothing but sin.

We cannot escape the many dangers of life without the real and constant help of God. Therefore, let's pray to Him continually. But how can we pray to Him without being with Him? How can we be with Him without thinking of Him often? And how can we think of Him often without forming a holy habit which keeps our thoughts with Him? You probably think I always say the same thing: well, it's true! For this is the best and easiest method I know; and since I use no other method, I advise all the world of it. We must know Him before we can love Him; and in order to know Him, we must think of Him often. When we keep coming to Him with a heart filled with love, then we will think of Him even more - our heart will remain with what we treasure. This reasoning deserves your careful consideration.

TENTH LETTER
THE TWENTY-NINETH OF OCTOBER, 1689

God must come first.

It has been difficult for me to write to Mr. N and I do it now only because you and Mrs. N have asked. If Mr. N can take advantage of the loss he has suffered, and put all his confidence in God, He will quickly give him another friend who is stronger and full of better intentions. God deals with hearts as He so chooses. Perhaps Mr. N is too attached to the friend he has lost. We should love our friends, but without hindering our love for God who must always come first.

I am very pleased with the trust you have placed in God. I pray that He increases it more and more. We can never place too much trust in such a good and faithful Friend. He will never fail us in this world or the next.

Please remember what I have recommended to you; think of God often, during the day and night, while you do your routine work, during time set for devotion, and even in your times of joyful relaxation. He is always near you and with you; never leave Him alone. Would you not think it rude to leave a friend alone who came to visit? Why then do we neglect God who resides in our heart? Do not forget Him, but think of Him often, love Him continually, and resolve to live and die in His presence. This is the glorious work of a Christian - this is our calling! If we do not know it naturally, then we must learn it. I will strive to assist you with my prayers and I remain yours in the Lord.

ELEVENTH LETTER
THE SEVENTEENTH OF NOVEMBER, 1690

Hold fast in suffering.

I do not pray for you to be delivered from your pains; but I earnestly pray that God would give you the strength and patience to bear them as long as He pleases. Take comfort with Him who holds you nailed to the cross: He will release you in His perfect timing. Blessed are they who suffer with Him. Grow accustomed to suffering in this manner and seek His strength to endure for as long as He determines is necessary. Do not be surprised that the world does not understand these truths; they can only suffer like what they are and not like Christians. They consider sickness as an affliction from nature and not as a blessing from God; and seeing it in this light, they find only grief and distress. But those who consider sickness as coming from the merciful hand of God, and the means He uses for their sanctification, find in it real happiness and comfort.

I wish you would be convinced that God is often nearer to us in our sickness than in our health. Rely on no other medicine than that which is directed by God; for He desires to be your cure. Put all your trust in Him and you will soon see the effects in you recovery. We often slow our healing by placing greater confidence in worldly remedies than in God. Any remedy you choose will only succeed as far as God permits; and when pains come from God, only He can cure them. He often sends diseases of the body to cure the diseases of the soul. Take comfort with the sovereign Physician of both the body and the soul.

You will most likely reply that I am very much at ease and dine at the table of the Lord. You have reason to say such things; but don't you think it would be painful for the greatest criminal in the world to eat at the King's table and be served

36

by Him, and, though he were greatly blessed, to be without the complete assurance of a pardon? The criminal would feel exceedingly great uneasiness and nothing could remove this anxiety except his trust in the goodness of his sovereign King.

So I assure you that whatever pleasures I taste at the table of my King, my sins are ever before my eyes as well as the lingering uncertainty of my forgiveness. I am tormented, though, in truth, the torment itself is pleasing since it reminds me to rely on faith.

Be satisfied in whatever condition God places you: however happy you think I am, I actually envy you. Pain and suffering would be a paradise to me if I could suffer with my God; and the greatest pleasure on earth would be hell if I attempted to enjoy them without Him; all my comfort would be to suffer something for His glory.

In a little while I must depart this world and go to God. My only comfort in this life is that I now truly see Him by faith. I see Him so clear that at times I might say, I do not just believe...I see! I experience what faith teaches and on that assurance I will live and die with Him.

Continue always with God: it is the only comfort and support for your affliction. I shall beg Him to be with you. I am in your service and yours in our Lord.

TWELFTH LETTER
THE TWENTY-EIGHTH OF NOVEMBER, 1690

Comfort through abiding faith.

If we were disciplined with abiding in the presence of God, all our times of sickness would seem light and momentary. God often permits us to suffer a little in order to purify our souls and exhort us to remain in Him.

Take courage! Continually offer Him your sufferings and pray for strength to endure them. Above all else, maintain the habit of abiding in the presence of God and forget Him as little as possible. Worship Him in your sickness and continue to offer yourself to Him; and when your suffering is at its worst, humbly ask Him, like a child with his loving father, to make you conformable to His holy will. I will assist you in this with my poor prayers.

God has many ways of drawing us to Himself and sometimes even hides Himself as a way of strengthening our faith. Our faith will never fail us in time of need; it alone should be our support and the foundation of our confidence which must only be in God.

I do not know what God intends to do with me. All the world may suffer, but I feel such continual joy that I can hardly contain myself. Though I deserve the greatest discipline, I remain continually blessed and am happy all the time.

I would willingly ask God to be part of your sufferings, but I know that in my great weakness I would be the most wretched man alive if He would leave me for even a moment. And yet, I do not know how He could ever leave me. My faith gives me an absolute assurance that He will never leave us, unless we first leave Him. Let's always remain in His presence and fear the thought of leaving Him. Let's resolve to live and die in His presence. Please pray for me as I pray for you.

THIRTEENTH LETTER

Exhortation for complete confidence in God.

I am distressed to see you suffer for this long. What gives me some consolation and softens the anguish I have regarding your grief, is that your sorrows are a proof of God's love toward you. If you can view your suffering in this light, you will bear them more easily. Given your present condition, I recommend that you abandon all human remedies and completely resign yourself to the will of God. It's possible He is waiting for that resignation and complete trust in Him before He cures you. Since all human remedies have already failed, you are not "tempting God" to abandon yourself into His hands and expect all from Him.

I told you in my last letter that He sometimes allows diseases of the body to cure the diseases of the soul. Therefore, have courage and ask God, not for deliverance from your pain, but for the strength to bear them for the love of Him alone - to bear as much as He desires for as long as He deems necessary.

Such a prayer is difficult for our human nature, but it is most pleasing to God and becomes exceedingly sweet when we focus on Him. Love sweetens all pain; and when we truly love God, we joyfully and courageously suffer for Him. I beg you to take your only comfort with Him who is the only true Physician for all your sickness.

He is the Father of the afflicted and always ready to help. He loves us infinitely more than we imagine. Let's therefore love Him in return and never seek our comfort elsewhere. I pray that you will soon receive His comfort. I will help you with my prayers, as poor as they are. I will always be yours in the Lord.

FOURTEENTH LETTER
THE TWENTY-SECOND OF JANUARY, 1691

Gratitude for mercies, consolation in suffering.

I give thanks to God for giving you some relief, as you desire. I have never been more content than these recent times I have been near death. I no longer pray for relief, but I pray for the strength to suffer with courage, humility, and love.

Oh, how sweet it is to suffer with God; no matter how great the sufferings may be, receive them with love. If we desire to enjoy the peace of paradise in this life, we must become accustomed to a familiar, humble, and loving communion with God. We must diligently keep our spirit from wandering and make our heart a spiritual temple where we can continually love Him. We should watch that we never do, say, nor think anything which may displease Him. When our minds are preoccupied with God, suffering will become full of Spiritual healing and comfort.

I know that it is initially difficult to arrive at this state; for we must act purely in faith. But, though it is difficult, we know we can do all things with the grace of God. He never refuses those who earnestly ask Him. Knock and keep on knocking, and I promise, that in His perfect timing, He will open and suddenly grant you all the blessings He has held back for years. Farewell. Pray for me as I pray for you. I hope to see Him soon.

FIFTEENTH LETTER
THE SIXTH OF FEBRUARY, 1691

Exhortation to deeper knowledge of God.

God knows best what we need, and all He does is for our good. If we really knew how much He loves us, we would always be ready to equally receive from His hand the sweet and the bitter; all would be pleasing that came from Him. The worst suffering never seems unbearable, except when we see them in the wrong light. When we see them in the hand of God - when we know it is our loving Father who dispenses the grief and suffering - all bitterness is removed and only comfort remains.

We should give all our thoughts to knowing God. The more we know Him, the more we desire to know Him. And since love is commonly measured by knowledge, our love for Him will be greater if we know Him deeper and more extensive; and if our love for God is great, we will love Him equally in our pain and in our pleasure.

Let's not be motivated to seek or love God for any of the blessings (no matter how great) which He has given or may give in the future. Such blessings cannot bring us as close to God as one simple act of faith. Let's seek Him often by faith; He is within us and we must not seek Him anywhere else. Are we not rude and deserving of great blame if we leave Him alone while we tend to trivial matters which do not please Him - and may even be offensive? It is fearful to consider how this wasted time will one day cost us dearly.

Let's begin to be earnestly devoted to Him and cast everything else out of our heart; He desires to reside there alone and without competition. Ask Him for His grace. If we do everything we can to remain in His presence, we will soon see the desired change for which we hope. I cannot thank Him enough for the relief He has given you. I pray He is merciful and allows me to see Him within the next few days. Let's commit to pray for one another.

[Brother Lawrence was confined to his bed just two days after writing this letter and died within the week.]

PART THREE

THE SPIRITUAL PRINCIPLES OF

BROTHER LAWRENCE

SPIRITUAL PRINCIPLES OF BROTHER LAWRENCE

All things are possible for him who believes, less difficult for him who hopes, more easy for him who loves, and still easier for him who perseveres in the practice of all three virtues. Our life's goal should be to become the most perfect worshippers of God we can possibly be - the worshipers we hope to be through all eternity.

1. We must be determined to always look to God and His glory in all we say and do. We should strive toward the goal of offering our lives to God as a perfect sacrifice of worship; this is what we hope to do for all eternity. We should firmly resolve to overcome, by God's grace, the many difficult trials we will encounter on our Spiritual walk.

2. When we begin on our Spiritual walk, we should thoroughly consider what we are, probing to the very depth of our heart. We will discover that we are deserving of all forms of contempt, unworthy of the name Christian. We are subject to all kinds of tribulations which distress us and impair the health of our soul, making us unstable in our moods, our behavior, and the disposition of our heart. In fact, we will discover we are people whom God will discipline and make humble by countless trials - internal as well as external.

3. We must firmly believe, without ever doubting, that God disciplines us for our good. He will send, as well as allow us to pass through, all forms of trials, for as long as He determines is necessary in order to bring our heart into complete submission; without which perfect devotion cannot exist.

4. The closer we draw to the perfect holiness of God, the more we realize our need for the grace of God; without His grace we can do nothing. This world, our flesh, and the devil join forces to wage a relentless assault on our soul. Without a humble reliance on the ever-present strength of God, these attacks would drag us down despite all our effort to resist. It

is difficult for our human nature to place complete dependence on God, but His grace makes it easy and brings us great joy and peace.

ESSENTIAL PRACTICES

1. The most holy and necessary practice in our Christian walk is to learn to live in the presence of God. We must discipline our soul to find its continual joy in His divine company, abiding with Him in humble and loving conversation during every moment of the day. We should remain in His presence, without following a set of rules or specific method, during all our times of temptation and trial, during times of dryness and distaste in our relationship with God, and even when we fall into times of unfaithfulness and sin.

2. We should continually apply ourselves to remaining in the presence of God. We should do this by making all of our simple actions become acts of loving communion with God, flowing naturally from the purity and simplicity of our heart.

3. We must do everything with thoughtful consideration without being impulsive or hurried, which are signs of an undisciplined spirit. We must do our work quietly, calmly, and lovingly, asking Him to bless the work of our hands. By keeping our heart and mind fixed on God, we will bruise the head of the devil and make his weapons fall to the ground.

4. When we are busy with our work, or thinking of spiritual things, or even during our established time of devotion when we lift up our voice in prayer, we should briefly, but as often as we can, worship God from the innermost part of our heart. We should take time to taste Him and touch Him, though only for a moment and in secret. Since we know that God is with us in all we do, that He resides in the very center of our soul, we should take every opportunity to praise and worship Him, to ask for His help, and to offer the fullness of our heart

with thanksgiving for all His many blessings.

What offering could be more acceptable to God than to quit the temporary things of this world and focus on the eternal by withdrawing to worship Him within the secret place of our soul. In doing this, we destroy the self-love which only exists when our senses are filled with input from the world; retreating for times of quiet will gradually free us from the world's pull. We offer God no greater sign of our faithfulness than when we turn away from created things and find our joy, though briefly, in the presence of the Creator.

However, I'm not saying we should completely turn our back on the world around us - that is impossible. You must be guided by good judgement; but I believe it is a common mistake in our Christian walk when we become too entangled in the world and fail to make the time to abandon all and worship Him from the innermost part of our soul and to rest in the peace and comfort of His presence even for a few brief moments. I have gotten a little off track, but I thought this subject needed further attention. Let's return to the essential practices.

5. All our acts of worship must be driven and guided by faith. We must truly believe that God lives within our soul, and that we must worship Him, love Him, and serve Him in Spirit and in truth; that He sees all - even the very secret places of our heart - the events of the past as well as those of the future; that he exists apart from everything and is dependent on nothing, but is the one to whom all creation depends; that He is infinite in perfection, absolutely sovereign, and deserves the complete surrender of our body and soul. We owe Him a debt of love we can never repay, but we make small payments as we give Him all our thoughts, words, and actions.

6. We must diligently examine ourselves to determine our strengths and weaknesses. We should understand the circumstances which most often cause us to stumble into sin. When we struggle, we should turn to God with complete confidence, abiding firmly in the presence of His divine

majesty, and in humble worship, we should present both our sorrows and our failures. In love, we should ask for His grace to help us in our need and to give us the strength to endure - in our weakness we will find His strength.

HOW TO WORSHIP IN SPIRIT AND IN TRUTH

1. To worship in Spirit and in truth means to worship Him as we should because God is a Spirit. We do this by presenting Him a true and humble spiritual worship from the innermost part of our heart. Only God can see this worship, and if we offer it without ceasing, it will become natural; as if God was one with our soul and our soul was one with Him. A disciplined practice will make this clear.

2. To worship God in truth means to recognize Him as who He really is, and to recognize ourselves as who we really are. We must sincerely believe that God is infinitely perfect, worthy of infinite love and worship, infinitely removed from sin, and likewise with every other divine attribute. It would be unreasonable if, after recognizing the majesty of God, we did not use all our strength and all our will to worship Him in the manner He is due.

3. Furthermore, to worship God in truth is to confess that we live completely contrary to His will; but that He desires to conform us into His image if we would only be willing. It is therefore unwise for us to ever turn away and withhold, even for a moment, the reverence, love, service, and unceasing worship that He most certainly deserves.

THE UNION OF THE SOUL WITH GOD

There are three levels of union with God. The first is general, the second is virtual, and the third is the actual union with God.

1. General union is the union our soul has with God simply and completely by His grace.

2. Virtual union is the condition of our soul as we begin an activity which leads us closer to God. The activity unites us with God, but only for as long as the activity lasts.

3. Actual union is a complete and perfect union in which the soul is awakened from its slumber and becomes intensely active. It becomes powerful, quicker than fire, brighter than the sun, and unhindered by passing clouds. Yet, our emotions can deceive us about this union. It is not defined by a brief feeling which causes us to say; "My God, I love You with all my heart," rather, it is a deeply spiritual, yet very simple, condition of the heart which fills us with a calm joy and a very humble and worshipful love for God. In this union, the soul is raised to heights where the love of God is so real that it cannot help but worship God and embrace Him with an indescribable tenderness. This love for God can only be understood through first hand experience.

4. Everyone who seeks union with God must understand that the will desires whatever causes it to be refreshed. We must recognize that God is far beyond our understanding; and to be united to Him, we must deny the will of all controlling pleasures so we can be free to love God above all other things. For if the will has any hope in understanding God, it can only be through love. There is a great difference between the desires of the will and its actual functioning. The desires of the will are contained within the confines of the soul, but the proper functioning flows through love and has its complete end in drawing closer to God.

THE PRESENCE OF GOD

1. The presence of God is the abiding as we direct our spirit to God; it is a realization that God is near - a realization which is given to us in our thoughts or in our actual understanding.

2. Through understanding, I have realized the presence of God for the past forty years. I refer to the presence of God by many other names; sometimes a simple act or a clear understanding of God; other times, a clear view through a window, a loving gaze, or an inner remembrance of Him; yet at other times, a patient waiting, a silent conversation, a confidence, or the life and peace of the soul. But all these terms and descriptions of the presence of God mean the same thing; His presence fills my soul in a very real and natural way.

3. By tireless effort and by constantly turning my thoughts to God, I have formed a habit that whether I'm busy at my job or peacefully at rest, my soul is lifted up above the things of this world and firmly dwells in the presence of God. This now occurs without much effort or thought and has become a place of true rest where my soul is full of joy - where faith is almost always my companion. This is the actual presence of God. When I abide in His presence, it feels as though only He and I are in the world and we talk without interruption: I ask Him to supply all my needs and He gives me fullness of joy.

4. We should understand that this communion with God takes place within the innermost part of our soul; for there is where we have the intimate conversation with God which results in a great and profound peace. Everything which happens on the outside concerns the soul no more than a flaming straw which quickly burns itself out; the cares of this world rarely disturb the true peace which is found within.

5. Returning to our discussion of the presence of God: you should know that God's tenderness and great loving-kindness

gradually ignites a fire within our soul, which so warmly holds it in a holy love for God that we are compelled to somewhat restrict the outward expression of our feelings.

6. We would be greatly surprised if we knew what conversation the soul actually had with God during these times. God seems to take such pleasure in this communion that when the soul continues to abide with Him, He pours out His blessings; and as if He fears that the soul might return to earthly concerns, He continues to bless until the soul finds a nourishment and joy unequalled by anything of this world - even beyond what the soul could possibly hope. God's blessings come without the soul doing anything but being willing to receive.

7. The presence of God is the life and nourishment of the soul; and with the help of God's grace, it can be achieved by diligent application of the method I will now describe.

HOW TO ENTER HIS PRESENCE

1. The first step is to live with purity. We should be careful not to do, say, or think anything which would be displeasing to God; and when we stumble, we should quickly repent and humbly ask His forgiveness.

2. The second step is to faithfully seek His presence by keeping the gaze of the soul firmly fixed on God. This should be done in clam faith and with a humble but total love, without allowing the cares of this world to enter and disturb our peace or cause anxiety.

3. We must be determined to look to God on all occasions - before we begin a task, engaging in the busyness of activity, and when a task is completed. This discipline requires great patience and practice; do not become discouraged! It will be difficult to form the habit of continual communion with God, but when it is properly formed, you will discover great joy.

The heart, which is the first thing in us to have life and has control over all the rest of the body, should be the first and the last to worship God, both at the beginning and the end of all Spiritual and bodily actions - the heart should worship throughout all the affairs of life. It is therefore in the heart where we should strive to make it a habit to "gaze" on God. We should simply, and without strain or much study, take the necessary steps to bring the heart into obedience.

4. For those who are determined to abide in the presence of God, I recommend offering God quiet words of the heart such as: "My God, I am wholly Yours. Oh God of love, I love You with all my heart. Lord, mold my heart as You desire; conform me to Your likeness." - or any similar words which are prompted by the heart at a particular moment. But be careful that your mind does not wander back again to the world with its temporal concerns. Keep your mind focused only on God, so that once it is controlled by the will, it will be constrained to abide in His presence.

5. Remaining in the presence of God is difficult at first, but if it is faithfully pursued, the discipline works secretly within the soul to produce the most marvelous effects. His presence allows an abundant flow of God's grace and gradually leads the soul to the ever-present vision of the loving and beloved God - this is the most holy, real, free, and life-giving manner of prayer and worship.

6. Remember that to remain in the presence of God, we must completely bring the senses under control since no soul which finds its joy in earthly things can find fullness of joy in His presence; to truly be with Him, we must let go of all attachments to things which are created.

BENEFITS OF THE PRESENCE OF GOD

1. The first benefit we receive from abiding in the presence of God is that our faith comes alive and active in all the events of our life. This is particularly true when we are in great need since, in abiding, we receive His grace when we are tempted and faced with times of trial. When we become accustomed to living by faith, it only takes a slight turn to see and feel that God is near; we can freely call on Him and, with assurance of His response, receive everything we need. As we grow in faith, we approach the state of being truly blessed - our faith continues to grow and the presence of God becomes so real that faith is swallowed up in sight and we can say; "I no longer just believe, I see and experience God."

2. Abiding in the presence of God makes us stronger in hope. Our hope grows in proportion to our knowledge of God; and when we abide, our faith penetrates the hidden mysteries of God and discovers in Him a beauty beyond comparison, infinitely surpassing anything of this world or of the most beautiful angels. Our hope continues to grow stronger, sustained and encouraged by the fullness of joy which it seeks and already has partially tasted.

3. When we hope in the eternal, our trust in earthly things is removed, and the will is ignited with the consuming fire of Divine love; for God's love is truly a consuming fire, completely burning to ash all that is contrary to His will. When the will has been ignited with His fire, we can no longer live except in His presence, and His presence creates within our heart a sacred eagerness, a holy love, and a violent passion to see God who is known, loved, served, and worshiped by all creation.

4. Through the discipline of abiding in the presence of God, by continually gazing on Him, we come to a full and deep knowledge of God - to an unclouded vision. All our life is spent in unceasing acts of love and worship, repentance

and trust, praise and prayer, service and sacrifice; at times life seems to be one long and unbroken time of communion in His presence.

5. I realize there are few who reach this level of continual intimacy; it is fully attained only be the grace of God which He only grants to a few. This unclouded vision is a gift from His hand; but it is a gift which He seldom denies to those who diligently seek His presence and earnestly desire His gift. And even if He does withhold the full measure of His grace, be assured that those who continually seek His presence will be granted sufficient grace to approach near to an unclouded vision and a joy which has no earthly comparison.

PART FOUR

THE CHARACTER OF BROTHER LAWRENCE

BY

JOSEPH DE BEAUFORT

THE CHARACTER OF BROTHER LAWRENCE

The power of His grace is no less great today than it was in the first days of the Church. God wished to keep saints for Himself until the end of the world. These saints would pay Him a respect worthy of His grandeur and majesty and would be models of virtue because of the holy example they set.

Such a man was Brother Lawrence of the Resurrection, a Carmelite lay-brother. God caused him to be born in these latter days to reverence Him and to provide an example of the faithful practice of all Godly virtues.

I am writing what I have personally seen and heard of the life of Brother Lawrence. He died about two years ago in the Carmelite Monastery in Paris and the memory of his life is still a sweet blessing.

Brother Lawrence chose to hold a very low position in the house of God rather than a lofty place among sinners. He took on the yoke of Jesus and preferred it to the empty show and pleasures of the world. He asked me to write down what I had collected of his thoughts and distribute them to those who had been freed from the chains of this world - I willing agree! And although I have already published a Eulogy and some letters of this good Brother, it seems we should take every opportunity to make known what we have preserved on this holy man. I firmly believe that I can do no greater good for society than to hold up this man as an example of solid devotion to God; and this in a time when almost everyone takes perverse ways to arrive at what they falsely define as good.

In these pages you will read many of Brother Lawrence's own words. I had several conversations with him and wrote down his words as soon as I left him. Nothing can present this servant of God better than his own words spoken from within the simplicity of his heart.

Though Brother Lawrence was completely devoted to God, he was also intensely human; he had an openness which won your confidence as soon as you met him - you immediately knew you had a friend whom you could trust. Once he knew you, he spoke freely and quickly demonstrated the great goodness of his heart. He spoke very simply, but to the point and full of good sense. Behind a rather rough exterior, there was a vastly perceptive mind beyond the normal reach of a man in his position; he had an insight which surpassed all expectations.

He was able to intelligently conduct himself in the most important matters, and give wise and safe counsel in all circumstances. These were the characteristics first seen by the ordinary observers.

He has already described the condition of his heart and the inner life of his soul in the four conversations I have previously presented. His conversion began with a high regard for the power and wisdom of God; and since the beginning, he has diligently sought to drive away all other thoughts besides his love for God.

Since this first realization of God was the beginning of his long journey of Spiritual growth, it is important to pause here and consider his initial conduct. Faith was the one and only light he took to light his path; not only did he first know God by faith, but he never desired to know God or His many ways other than by faith. He often said that all he heard others say, all he found in books, and all he had written himself, seemed tasteless and dull when compared with what faith had revealed to him about the unspeakable riches of God and Jesus Christ. "He alone can reveal His true nature. We seek to find Him through intellectual reasoning and science, forgetting that in these we only can see a poor copy - all the while, we neglect to cast our gaze on the most excellent original. God reveals Himself in the innermost depths of our soul, but we fail to know Him because we refuse to look where He may be found. We leave Him to spend our time with trivial matters and effectively scorn our communion with Him Who is ever-present - Him Who is our King!

"It is not enough to know God as a theory, formed simply by what we read in books, or by some temporary emotion or wave of inspiration; we must make faith come alive and, through faith, rise above all passing emotions to worship the Father and Jesus Christ in all their divine perfection. This path of faith is the Spirit of the Church and is fully sufficient for our journey."

Not only did Brother Lawrence perceive God as present in his soul by faith, but in all the activities of his life he would immediately raise his heart to God and seek His presence.

He had seen a leafless tree in winter which he knew would flower and bear fruit in the spring; this had given him such a solid vision of God, that after forty years it was as clear and real as when he first received it. Throughout his life, he continued to use visual examples of the world to lead him to the unseen things of eternity.

Brother Lawrence preferred to read the Bible more than any other book; he found he could grow in his faith more simply and purely with the words of Jesus Christ. He was resolved from the very beginning to pursue a deep sense of the presence of God by what he saw through faith. He continued to glorify God and express his love in every activity; asking for God's help before he began and giving thanks when he was finished. He would confess his shortcomings and areas of neglect, and calmly ask for God's forgiveness without making excuses and with complete assurance of God's favorable response. This communion with God occurred throughout all his daily activities and, without being the slightest bit distracting, provided assistance with every step and allowed him to accomplish his tasks with greater ease.

He confessed that this practice had been difficult in the beginning, many times his mind had wandered from God; but after humble confession of his failure, he returned without much trouble or concern. There were times when his mind would be invaded by a multitude of undisciplined thoughts which would violently take possession of the place of God.

When this would happen he remained calm and, simply but quickly, removed the invading thoughts and returned to his communion with God. His faithfulness and patience was eventually rewarded with an unbroken and undisturbed sense of the presence of God deep within his soul. All his numerous and varied acts of faith were changed into an unclouded vision, an enlightened love and uninterrupted joy.

He once said: "My time of great busyness is no different than my time of prayer; in the noise and clatter of the kitchen, while many people are asking me things at the same time, I maintain the presence of God as peacefully as when I'm on my knees during our formal time of communion. Sometimes, my faith becomes so clear that I think I may have lost it. Normally, our Spiritual vision appears to be in the process of being cleared; but there comes a day which is without clouds and without end - the glorious day of the life to come." This is the height to which faithfulness led our good Brother - a faithfulness which allowed him to leave all other thoughts behind and be set free for unbroken communion with God. This habit had become so natural that it was now impossible to turn away from God and become entangled with other matters.

In one of our conversations, he pointed out that the presence of God is reached more by the heart and love than through understanding: "In the way of God thoughts count for little, but love is everything. It is not necessary to do great things; rather, we can do all our little acts for the love of God. I turn my eggs that are frying in the pan for the love of God; and when that is done, if there is nothing else for me to do, I give myself fully to Him in worship - praising the One who gave me the grace to work. Afterward I am happier than a king; for I am content to simply pick up a straw from the ground for the love of God.

"We search for various methods to teach us how to love God. These methods of searching for a sense of the presence of God do little more than clutter our minds and cause great trouble. The presence of God is found much easier by simply doing everything for the love of God - by making all of our daily tasks an offering of pure and holy love - and in this manner, developing a sense of His presence through the communion of our heart with His. We don't need special studies to 'enlighten' us as to the 'proper' method; we simply come as we are and take everything to Him in love - this must be the single focus of our heart."

However, we cannot assume that to properly love God we only need to offer Him our actions, ask for His help, and produce acts of love. Brother Lawrence only reached his high degree of continual love because of the discipline he maintained from the beginning to do nothing against the will of God and because he turned his back on all controlling pulls of the flesh for the sake of loving God. "Since entering the monastery and devoting myself fully to God, I no longer concern myself with thoughts of my morality or of my Salvation. Through many years of drawing near to God and abiding in His presence, I have come to understand that my only purpose in life is to live as though there was no one else besides myself and God in all the world."

Therefore, Brother Lawrence began by abandoning everything for God and doing everything for His love. He completely forgot himself and no longer thought about heaven or hell, or past sins, or, after he confessed and asked God's forgiveness, the sins he committed every day. Once he confessed his sins, he never allowed his mind to go back to the offense; rather, he gave himself to God and entered into His peace where he intended to remain for life and death, for time and eternity. "We are made for God and for Him alone; He therefore never thinks it wrong to abandon everything, even ourselves, to be fully devoted to Him. In the presence of God, we are able to see what we lack better than any amount of self examination which only yields the remnant. Our self examination is always full of self-love and, under the delusion of striving toward our own perfection, we keep our focus on our self instead of lifting our eyes and heart to God."

Brother Lawrence often said that during the four years of

trial, when no one could remove the great burdening sense that he was lost, he never wavered from his first resolution. Instead of worrying about what was in his future or about his present anguish, he would comfort himself with thoughts such as: "No matter what happens to me, I will live all my remaining days doing everything for the love of God." In forgetting his concerns about self, Brother Lawrence had found truth in God.

He said he had found, deep within his soul, a love for the will of God that took the place of the love we normally have for our own will; in all the events of life, he clearly saw the working of God's divine plan. This kept him in perfect peace because, in all things, his mind remained on God. He was never surprised when told of any great evil in the world; rather, he said he was amazed there was not more when he considered the deep, dark pit into which sin will lead a man. He would lift his heart to God, and seeing that God could remedy the situation but chose to allow the evil to continue, for reasons useful to the working of His plan, he would earnestly pray for the sinner and continue in His peace without being distressed.

Without warning, I once told him that an important matter for which he had worked very hard could not be accomplished because of a resolution made by his Superiors. He simply replied; "We must believe they have a good reason for their decision. Our duty now is to obey and say no more about it." And this he did. Although he had several opportunities to speak on the matter, he never once opened his mouth.

Once when Brother Lawrence was very sick, a man of high standing within the religious community came to visit. He asked our good Brother if God would allow him to choose, would he rather live a little longer and grow in holiness, or die now and be immediately received into heaven. Without hesitation, he replied that he would leave the choice to God; that he would do nothing but wait in peace until God revealed His perfect will.

This attitude brought him perfect freedom and allowed

him to be unconcerned about specific events of the world. He had no bias toward any party and no trace of self-preference could be found in his character, nor any prejudice which naturally arises from an attachment to country or culture. He was equally loved by those who had a completely opposite temperament and, in turn, he wished well for everyone without regard for who they were or what they believed. As a Citizen of Heaven, he was not bound by any chains to the earth; his view was no longer constrained by time. After long contemplation of God and seeking the presence of Him Who is Eternal, his mind had been eternally renewed.

Everything was the same to him, every situation and every task. He found God everywhere, as close while in the humblest activity as when praying with all the members of the monastery. He found no urgent need for retreats, since he met the same God to love and worship in his common tasks as in the stillness of the desert.

His only method of going to God and abiding in His presence was to do everything for the love of Him. It did not matter what activity he was doing, provided that in whatever he did he sought to glorify God. He looked only to Him and not to the specific work. He knew that the more the task was against his natural inclination, the greater the love which made him sacrifice his will to God. The smallness of the work did not reduce the value of the offering in the slightest, for God does not regard the greatness of the work, but the love with which it is accomplished.

Another quality of Brother Lawrence's character was his great firmness of mind - a firmness which might be called fearlessness in another walk of life. This firmness gave evidence of a soul which had risen far above the fears and hopes of the world. He marveled at nothing, was astonished by nothing, and feared nothing. This wonderful stability came from the same source as the rest of his Godly character. The high notion of God gave him, deep within his heart, a perfect picture of his Creator in all His sovereign justice and infinite mercy. This view of God assured him that God would never deceive him, and would send only things which were good for him. On his part, he was resolved to never grieve God, but to do all and endure all for the love of Him.

One day I asked him who was his Director. He said that he had none and believed he didn't need one since the rules and duties he had as a monk dictated everything related to outward concerns, and the Gospel dictated an inner life of loving God with all his heart. With these as his guide, a Director didn't seem necessary - but he felt a great desire for a Confessor.

Those who receive no guidance in their Spiritual life except from the way they feel and how they are inclined, who think they only need to examine themselves as to whether they feel devoted or not, will never have Spiritual stability nor a solid foundation. Our dispositions and feelings continually change, sometimes because of our own neglect, and sometimes by God's direction. He varies His gifts and manner of dealing with us according to our needs.

Our Brother, on the other hand, remained firmly on the path of faith which never changes. He was stable and constant because his focus was always to carry out whatever tasks God gave him to do in whatever location He had placed him. He saw no value in the actual task other than in being obedient and doing all to bring glory and honor to God. Instead of examining his inclinations and feelings, or testing the path he was walking, he fixed his eyes on God; he "raced" toward the goal of the presence of God by daily acts of meekness, righteousness, and love. He kept himself busy with doing his tasks for the love of God rather than thinking about the specific task he was doing.

The devotion of Brother Lawrence, resting on this solid foundation, was not dependent on wild ideas or experiences. He was convinced that even that which is genuine is most often a sign of weakness within the soul - a sign that the soul has found contentment in God's gift rather than in God Himself. Except for the earliest days in the monastery, none of these experiences were part of his life - at least he never mentioned anything to any of his closest friends.

Throughout his life, he followed in the steps of the Saints, along the sure and certain way of faith. He never strayed from the beaten track, the well trodden path of sanctification, and continued in the exercise of what the Church has declared from the beginning - all else he viewed with distrust. His great common-sense and the light given by his simple faith warned him of the hidden rocks on which so many become shipwrecked in their Spiritual life; they let themselves drift along the current of curiosity and imagination, of love of novelty and human guidance.

Prepared by such a life, Brother Lawrence saw death approach without distress. He had great patience throughout his life, but it grew even stronger as he approached the end. He was never the least bit concerned when his body was overcome with pain and sickness; his countenance was full of joy and even more so his speech - so much so that those who visited needed to ask whether or not he was suffering.

"Forgive me," he replied. "Yes, I suffer. The pain in my side gives me great trouble, but my spirit is happy and content." They then asked, "Suppose God requires you to suffer for ten more years, what then?" Without hesitation, he calmly said; "I will suffer, not only for ten years, but until the Day of Judgement, if it is God's will; and I would hope He would continue to assist me with His grace so I could bear it joyfully."

As the last hour of his life approach, he frequently cried out, "Oh faith, faith!" This was a better expression of his life than any long speech. His worship of God never ceased: he told a fellow Brother that he hardly needed faith any longer to realize the presence of God - his faith had grown so strong that faith had been swallowed up by what he saw and experienced of God. He was so bold as he approached that dark valley that he told a friend he feared neither death nor hell, neither the judgement of God nor the attacks of the devil.

His words were so full of comfort and grace that many of

the Brothers in the monastery came to speak with him and ask questions. One of them asked if he knew how terrible it was to fall into the hands of the living God, since no one knows for sure if he deserves God's love; "I agree," said Brother Lawrence, "but I do not wish to know if I'm deserving, for fear of my pride swelling up and consuming me; no, we can do nothing better than to completely, and continually, abandon ourselves to God."

After he had received the Last Sacraments, a Brother asked him if he was at peace and what was occupying his mind. He replied: "I am doing what I will continue to do through all eternity - blessing God, praising God, worshiping God, and giving Him the full love of my heart. My Brother's, our one and only business is to worship and love Him, without thought of anything else."

These were his last words. He died the next day, February 12th, 1691, at nine o'clock in the morning. He died without any pain or struggle, with the same calm tranquility that characterized the last forty years of his life. Our dear Brother truly lived and died while in the presence of God.

PART FIVE

DEVOTIONS FOR
LIVING IN THE PRESENCE OF GOD

BY

STEVE TROXEL

STRAIN TOWARD THE VINE

The writings of Paul present a wonderful perspective of the Christian life. Paul states; "it is by grace you have been saved, through faith," (Ephesians 2:8). But Paul also sets a high standard regarding sin; "Do not let sin reign in your mortal body so that you obey its evil desires," (Romans 6:12). Though holiness will not earn our Salvation, we are definitely called to live a holy life.

We are called to be holy even though we continue to fall short of God's standard. Paul therefore refers to our life after Salvation as a race driven toward a goal; "Forgetting what is behind and straining toward what is ahead, I press on toward the goal to win the prize for which God has called me," (Philippians 3:12-14).

This can be a wonderful motivator as we picture a well-conditioned athlete straining toward the finish line. However, if we press and strain toward the wrong goal - or even toward the right goal but with our own strength - we will soon become greatly fatigued and discouraged. Yes, we are in a race; but we must not allow the world to establish the rules of the race or determine the finish line. This is an event in which the world has no experience nor understanding.

Two thousand years ago, Jesus clearly defined the goal to which we are striving; "This is to my Father's glory, that you bear much fruit," (John 15:8). Fortunately, Jesus also showed us how to produce fruit and attain our goal.

John 15:4-5

"Remain in Me, and I will remain in you. No branch can bear fruit by itself; it must remain in the vine. Neither can you bear fruit unless you remain in Me. I am the vine; you are the branches. If a man remains in Me and I in him, he will bear much fruit; apart from Me you can do nothing."

In our Christian walk, we are to produce fruit by bringing glory and honor to God in all we do; a life lived in holiness is one type of fruit. However, fruit can only grow if we remain intimately attached to the vine. A branch cannot produce anything by itself - we cannot produce holiness or anything else esteemed by God - but if the branch remains connected and allows the life of the vine to flow through its veins, it WILL produce much fruit.

Let's attach firmly to the vine of Jesus Christ by keeping our eyes, as well as our thoughts, firmly fixed on Him, and allow nothing but His life to flow though our veins. Let's live each day in the presence of God and produce baskets of fruit for His glory and honor. Let's continue to run and strain - but let's run and strain toward the vine.

THE MOUNTAIN OF FAITH

When Abraham was over eighty years old, God made him a wonderful promise: "A son coming from your own body will be your heir. Look up at the heavens and count the stars - so shall your offspring be," (Genesis 15:4-5).

Many years went by without any indication that God would fulfill this promise. Finally, when Abraham was one hundred and his wife, Sarah, was ninety, God fulfilled His promise through the birth of Isaac. But when Isaac was a young boy, God told Abraham to sacrifice his beloved son.

Genesis 22:2

"Take your son, your only son, Isaac, whom you love, and go to the region of Moriah. Sacrifice him there as a burnt offering on one of the mountains I will tell you about."

Abraham didn't even question the apparent conflict between God's promise and His command - he simply obeyed. He took Isaac and climbed the mountain, placed him on top of a pile of wood, and "took the knife to slay his son," (Genesis 22:10). Not only was Abraham about to sacrifice his only son, he was also ending the hope of God's promise being fulfilled.

Through this unimaginable trial, Abraham never seemed anxious or concerned - his faith never seemed to waiver.

As Abraham was about to kill his son, God stopped him and provided a substitute sacrifice; "Abraham went over and took the ram and sacrificed it as a burnt offering instead of his son," (Genesis 22:13). But why did God put Abraham through such a test of his faith?

The test wasn't for God - He already knew Abraham's faith! The test may have been for Abraham to see the strength of his own faith, but Abraham already seemed confident - he already seemed to know. If not for God or Abraham, then why? It's possible the sole reason Abraham climbed the mountain, and put his faith to the test, was so we could see a real demonstration of the faith to which each of us are called.

God is calling us to a life of faith where we have such a strong assurance of His presence that He is all we need...all we value and hold dear. If there are things of this world to which we still cling - things which we can't imagine ever letting go - then there is still distance between us and God and we continue to miss out on His very best. The real blessings from God come when we give ourselves completely to Him, without ANY reservation. Let's give Him ALL our heart and be willing to sacrifice ALL for His glory and honor. Let's, once and for all, climb the mountain of faith.

RESOLVE TO BE TRANSFORMED

What will we do different in this next year? Each year, we make resolutions to exercise more, eat less, stop habits, start habits, and take various steps to become "self-improved."

As we examine ourselves and look for changes we can make to become the man or woman we desire to be, let's focus some of our effort on the changes which have eternal significance. Jesus said it well as He admonished the Pharisees for their hypocrisy: "You clean the outside of the cup and dish, but inside they are full of greed and self-indulgence. First clean the inside...and then the outside also will be clean," (Matthew 23:25-26).

Unless we focus on the condition of our heart - the closeness of our relationship with our Heavenly Father, our love for Him and our desire to be with Him always - we will never achieve the desired change; the true and permanent change which is the peace and contentment found only in the presence of God.

Romans 12:2

"Do not conform any longer to the pattern of this world, but be transformed by the renewing of your mind. Then you will be able to test and approve what God's will is - His good, pleasing and perfect will."

The renewing of our mind is an inward change whereby we are "conformed to the likeness of His Son," (Romans 8:29). It's a process of changing our thoughts, priorities, and goals to be aligned with those of Christ: "Let this mind be in you, which was also in Christ Jesus," (Philippians 2:5 KJV). The mind of Christ was pure, focused on the Father, and determined to do His will: "My food is to do the will of Him who sent Me and to finish His work," (John 4:34).

On our list of things to do different in this next year, I pray we include more time with God in prayer, more time in His Word; more time loving Him with ALL our heart, seeking His presence, and earnestly desiring to know, and do, His will. Let our prayer for one another be that we draw ever closer to our Heavenly Father and experience His love new and fresh every day. In the coming days, months and years - however many we may still have - let's make changes which will last for all eternity: let's resolve to be transformed!

KNOW HIM BETTER

When a child is born into a family, there is almost an instant bond. The parent sees the newborn as precious and the newborn "sees" the parent as a place of comfort and security. As parent and child spend time together, the child begins to know the face and trust the voice of "Ma-Ma" and "Da-Da." The relationship is close and the child relies on the parent to meet ALL their needs.

However, as the child grows, commitments with activities and friends begin to limit the time with parents. In the search for independence, there is often rebellion toward parental instruction and counsel. Soon, the parent and child drift apart and no longer communicate as they once had; they no longer understand each other's needs - they no longer know one another.

Ephesians 1:16-17

"I have not stopped giving thanks for you, remembering you in my prayers. I keep asking that the God of our Lord Jesus Christ, the glorious Father, may give you the Spirit of wisdom and revelation, so that you may know Him better."

Notice that this is Paul's continuous prayer; that we be given revelation and wisdom. Revelation is the "unveiling" of God's truth and wisdom is the application of this truth in our lives. Both of these serve a single purpose; each are used to draw us closer and become more intimate by knowing Him better.

As we continue to grow and mature in our relationship with Jesus Christ, there is a tendency to hit those Spiritual teenage years where we have things pretty well figured out - or so we think. We begin to gain self confidence and start to trust in our own ability. We get more and more involved in activities (maybe even "good" activities) and with friends (maybe even "good" friends). One day we wake up and find we've drifted. We didn't intentionally walk away, but we no longer feel the passion - we no longer really know God.

As a loving father longs to hold his child, our Heavenly Father longs for us to draw near to Him, love Him, and know Him; "Let him who boasts boast about this: that he understands and knows Me," (Jeremiah 9:24). God's Word always speaks about "knowing" someone as being a very personal and intimate relationship: "Adam knew his wife; and she conceived, and bare Cain," (Genesis 4:1 KJV). Our relationship with God must be so close that nothing is hidden and nothing is held back; He deserves ALL our love.

The best way to know someone better is to spend time together. No matter how busy we get, we must continue to come into the presence of God, talk with Him in prayer, and listen to Him through the reading and quiet reflection of His Word. Let's commit (or recommit) to love God with all our heart, soul, mind, and strength. Let's draw near to God and continually seek to know Him better.

AN ANXIOUS HEART

Being anxious or having anxiety is defined as being mentally troubled with worry or concern. Unfortunately, we have been battling with anxiety as part of our nature ever since Adam ate the forbidden fruit and tried in vain to hide from God (Genesis 3:8-10). The negative effects of anxiety were understood three thousand years ago when King Solomon wrote his proverbs of wisdom.

Proverbs 12:25

"An anxious heart weighs a man down, but a kind word cheers him up."

Anxiety was still part of our nature when Paul was preaching the Good News of Jesus. Almost in the same breath that Paul instructs us to "Rejoice in the Lord always!" (Philippians 4:4), he teaches on removing anxiety from our life.

Philippians 4:6

"Do not be anxious about anything, but in everything, by prayer and petition, with thanksgiving, present your requests to God."

When we find ourself being overly concerned or mentally troubled about ANYTHING, we must go to God (with thanksgiving) and give our burdens to Him. This doesn't mean we ignore our problems, but we must learn to view the things of this world against the backdrop of eternity. The concerns of this life always fade as we compare them to the eternal glory of His Kingdom.

Matthew 6:25,34

"Therefore I tell you, do not worry {or be anxious} about your life, what you will eat or drink; or about your body, what you will wear. Is not life more important than food, and the body more important than clothes? But seek first His Kingdom and His righteousness, and all these things will be given to you as well."

Faith must be the solid foundation of our life; when we really believe that; "in all things God works for the good of those who love Him," (Romans 8:28), it becomes difficult to be concerned as the events of our life unfold - we simply continue to love.

Therefore, our level of worry is a good indicator of our level of trust - our level of belief. As we draw closer to God, our eyes are opened and we see that He has given (and will continue to give) all we really need.

When we feel weighed down, pressured, or stressed - when concerns are coming in fast motion from all directions and we don't know where to begin - we must stop and take a long, deep breath! We must refocus on Jesus and His Word. We must be reminded of eternity in the presence of a loving God and diligently seek His Kingdom (His presence). We will then receive His gift of peace and will no longer live burdened with the weight of an anxious heart.

IN HIS COURTS

Once we enter through the gate of Jesus Christ (John 10:9), by believing in Him for the forgiveness of our sins, we have dramatically altered our eternity. We were once blind and destined to be separated from God in Hell, but now we "see" and will spend eternity as His child in Heaven.

After we pass through the Gate, God sets a plan in motion for us to be "conformed to the likeness of His Son," (Romans 8:29). God's plan is for us to be transformed into people whose sole desire is to bring Him glory, and praise His name forever.

At times, this process can be very painful as we strip away layers of pride and crawl from under the dominion of our old sinful nature. But as we persevere and catch a glimpse of His glory, we will never again desire to be away from His presence.

Psalm 84:10

"Better is one day in Your courts than a thousand elsewhere; I would rather be a doorkeeper in the house of my God than dwell in the tents of the wicked."

A single day in the presence of God is better than a thousand days anywhere else - better than ANYTHING this world can offer. If we do not believe this truth, we have not yet been in His presence - we have not yet tasted the sweet fruit of His Spirit.

Look again at the passion in the second part of the above passage: "I would rather be an insignificant doorman in the house of God than reside in the largest mansion while living in wickedness," (my paraphrase). This passion to be in the presence of God is also recorded earlier.

Psalm 84:2

*"My soul yearns, even faints, for the courts of the Lord;
my heart and my flesh cry out for the living God."*

Our Heavenly Father longs for us to have this passion in our life. "Enter His gates with thanksgiving and His courts with praise," (Psalm 100:4). God's holy temple - His place of worship - now resides within every believer....resides within us! (1 Corinthians 3:16). Let's fill His temple with praise by worshiping Him every moment of our day from the innermost parts of our heart - let's passionately spend EVERY moment in His courts.

HIS GENTLE WHISPER

Elijah was a prophet to the northern kingdom of Israel and was used by God to demonstrate His almighty power against the four hundred and fifty prophets of Baal. But even after witnessing God's hand move through him, Elijah fled into the desert the moment his life was threatened; "I have had enough Lord; take my life," (1 Kings 19:4).

God demonstrated great compassion as He sent an angel to comfort Elijah and help him regain his strength. He then sent Elijah on a forty day journey through the desert - a journey which ended at the same mountain where Moses received The Ten Commandments. When confronted by God on the mountain, Elijah honestly expressed his discouragement: "The Israelites have rejected Your covenant... I am the only one left, and now they are trying to kill me too." (1 Kings 19:8).

Elijah felt utterly alone. He understood the holiness of God and how far his people had strayed from God's path; but he also felt overwhelmed and helpless, unable to make a significant impact on God's Kingdom. God answered Elijah by calling him to "stand on the mountain in the presence of the Lord." (1 Kings 19:11).

1 Kings 19:11-13

"Then a great and powerful wind tore the mountains apart and shattered the rocks before the Lord, but the Lord was not in the wind. After the wind there was an earthquake, but the Lord was not in the earthquake. After the earthquake came a fire, but the Lord was not in the fire. And after the fire came a gentle whisper. When Elijah heard it, he pulled his cloak over his face."

Every one of us who desire to walk God's path and serve Him with all our heart will sooner or later relate to Elijah. It's unfortunate, but many will face Elijah's overwhelming helplessness time and time again; the task at hand is simply too great when we only consider our limited ability. But God's solution is always the same; we must come into His presence, be clothed with His strength, and listen intently for His leading.

We often assume that when the Creator of The Universe desires to "speak," it will be with an earth shattering and thundering call; "Walk this way!" But God desires for our heart, soul, mind, and strength to be focused on Him; to be free of the clutter and noise; to be free of the distractions which tend to "choke the word, making it unfruitful," (Mark 4:19). So it's not surprising that God most often speaks to us in a whisper during the quiet and still moments of our life.

No matter how busy we become, we must set aside time which is quiet and undisturbed - time where we can enter into the presence of God, worship Him, and listen. We will eventually be able to enter God's presence without regard to our external surroundings, but in the beginning we must find moments of quiet. God desires to encourage us and give us clear direction today. Let's love Him with all our heart and listen intently for His gentle whisper.

OPEN OUR EYES

The king of Aram was at war with Israel - but every time he moved his army, the prophet Elisha would inform the Israelites. The king concluded that the only way to win the war would be to eliminate Elisha; "'Go, find out where he is,' the king ordered, 'so I can send men and capture him,'" (2 Kings 6:13).

When the king found where Elisha was staying, he sent his army to surround the city. When Elisha's servant woke and saw the army, he became very frightened: "Oh, my lord, what shall we do?" (2 Kings 6:15); but Elisha comforted his servant by allowing him to see the real battle.

2 Kings 6:16-17

"'Don't be afraid,' the prophet answered. 'Those who are with us are more than those who are with them.' And Elisha prayed, 'O Lord, open his eyes so he may see.' Then the Lord opened the servant's eyes, and he looked and saw the hills full of horses and chariots of fire all around Elisha."

Our false perception is the biggest cause of fear; in fact, we might boldly say it's the only cause! If we live without faith, our perception is strictly limited to what we see with our eyes; but as our faith and understanding of God increase, we are able to trust in what we cannot see and live in peace. We are able to live with the calm assurance that "the One who is in you is greater than the one who is in the world," (1 John 4:4).

Battles occur in and around us every day - battles which cause us to become burdened and discouraged. We desire to walk down God's path, but the pulls and attacks of the world seem relentless. Remember that the battle we see with our physical eyes is never the real battle: "For our struggle is not against flesh and blood," (Ephesians 6:12). Our spouse, parents, children, or co-workers are not the enemy - neither is our health or finances. These temporal things are not the true cause of our pain nor should they be the source of our joy - the battle is Spiritual, and we're not alone!

We should be greatly comforted today: "Those who are with us are more than those who are with them." Let's draw near to God until we catch a glimpse of how much He loves us - and how much He is fighting for us. The ultimate battle has already been won! We must now trust Him and give Him every portion of our heart; in turn, He will pour out His blessings with a greater abundance than we could ever hope! Heavenly Father, we desire to see You clearly today - draw us into Your presence...and open our eyes!

CONSIDER WHAT WE SACRIFICE

By the time Jeremiah became a prophet, the people of Israel had occupied the land of Canaan for about eight hundred years. Those many years were characterized by a continuing rejection of God - time and again the people turned from God and embraced the gods of the world.

Through Jeremiah, God pleaded for His people to return and worship Him as the One True God: "Tell them everything I command you; do not omit a word. Perhaps they will listen and each will turn from his evil way," (Jeremiah 26:2-3).

God's character is wonderfully revealed in the writings of Jeremiah. We can almost feel God's heart breaking as He tells Jeremiah how far His children have fallen.

Jeremiah 19:4-5

"For they have forsaken Me and made this a place of foreign gods; they have burned sacrifices in it to gods that neither they nor their fathers nor the kings of Judah ever knew. They have built the high places of Baal to burn their sons in the fire as offerings to Baal - something I did not command or mention, nor did it enter My mind."

When God first led the Israelites out of Egypt, He warned them about following the practices of the local people: "You must not do as they do in the land of Canaan, where I am bringing you," (Leviticus 18:3). The ways of the world will always be in conflict with the ways of God.

God's chosen people not only turned their backs, they became involved in a local form of "worship" that included sacrificing their own children. It's almost as if God was shaking His head in disbelief...I wonder if He's still shaking His head today.

We have been blessed with family, friends, and a wonderful relationship with God through the forgiveness of Jesus. And yet, how often do we sacrifice these blessings to the gods of this world? How often do we follow the practices of the world and burn our children or marriage in the fire of materialism; how often do we sacrifice our relationships on the altar of selfish pleasure?

Our Heavenly Father is calling us to a Spiritual worship of complete sacrifice: "Offer your bodies as living sacrifices, holy and pleasing to God," (Romans 12:1). This sacrifice is one of continually releasing our will in order to be "poured out as a drink offering," (2 Timothy 4:6). Let's bring our very best to God's table and worship Him with a pure and complete devotion; let's take a hard look at where we spend our time and what consumes our thoughts - let's carefully consider what we sacrifice.

FULL MEASURE OF OUR HEART

When God gave the Law to Moses, He specified rules for worship and rules for how people should treat one another. When Jesus was asked to state the most important commandment, He replied: "Love the Lord your God will all your heart and with all your soul and with all your mind and with all your strength," (Mark 12:30). At another point in His ministry, Jesus taught that the Law and the Prophets are summed up as you "do to others what you would have them do to you," (Matthew 7:12). But our love for God and love for others must be complete and true.

God demands honesty in His people. "You must have accurate and honest weights and measures. For the Lord detests anyone who deals dishonestly," (Deuteronomy 25:15-16). Jesus emphasized the use of fair measurement standards as He taught His disciples.

Luke 6:38

"Give, and it will be given to you. A good measure, pressed down, shaken together and running over, will be poured into your lap. For with the measure you use, it will be measured to you."

Jesus Christ died for the forgiveness of our sins so we might receive "the blessing given to Abraham," (Galatians 3:14). This blessing includes the right to be called children of God and the inheritance of eternal life, but it also extends to our days on earth as we receive the blessings of true joy, peace, and contentment.

It should not be surprising that the measure of blessing we receive from God is directly related to the measure we use to give unto Him. This measure has little to do with the amount or "value" of the gifts we bring: "To obey is better than sacrifice and to heed is better than the fat of rams," (1 Samuel 15:22). We can't "purchase" our blessings; rather, the measure we use to give unto God is in our worship, our love, and our obedience. Our measure is in our desire to walk every moment of our day in His presence and praise Him with every breath.

Our dealings with God become dishonest and deceitful when we expect a full measure of His blessing of peace, His blessing of clear direction, or even His blessing of assurance, and yet cheat Him with every measure we return. There is only one way to receive the full measure of God's blessing; we must first praise Him and give Him the full measure of our worship - we must follow wherever He leads and bless Him with the full measure of our heart.

THE LOOK OF HOLINESS

During the week before He was crucified, Jesus was asked many questions by the religious leaders. However, their questions were never asked for the purpose of education or to satisfy their curiosity, they were asked with the intent of finding fault; "The Pharisees went out and laid plans to trap Him in His words," (Matthew 22:15). Jesus answered each of their questions, but then He warned the crowds about the hypocrisy of those who were trying to trap Him.

Matthew 23:5-6

> *"Everything they do is done for men to see: They make their phylacteries wide and the tassels on their garments long; they love the place of honor at banquets and the most important seats in the synagogues."*

The phylactery was a small box containing scripture and was worn on the forehead or arm to fulfill the command of God as given through Moses: "Fix these words of mine in your hearts and minds; tie them as symbols on your hands and bind them on your foreheads," (Deuteronomy 11:18).

The Pharisees strictly followed the Law of Moses, but they also followed many self-created rules. Jesus never condemned them for following these rules, but He greatly questioned the condition of their heart. The Pharisees had forgotten that the purpose of everything they did was to worship God; they focused on their appearance as they sought to look holy and obtain the approval of men.

This problem was not new to the time of Jesus. Over seven hundred years earlier, the people of Israel had lost their heart for worship: "These people come near to Me with their mouth and honor Me with their lips, but their hearts are far from Me. Their worship of Me is made up only of rules taught by men," (Isaiah 29:13).

Unfortunately, this problem is still rampant today. We've created a list of do's and don'ts, and consider ourselves "worshipers" when we properly follow the list. We define our closeness with God by our church attendance, our service to others, or even our time spent reading His Word. But all these "good" and worthwhile actions do not define our relationship - they do not define our worship! "Man looks at the outward appearance, but the Lord looks at the heart," (1 Samuel 16:7).

Everything we do must be motivated by love with a desire to praise and honor our Heavenly Father. Our religious acts mean absolutely nothing if not accompanied by a heart full of love and thanksgiving. Let's become true worshipers who express our love for God in everything we do and say! Let's never allow our lives to be driven by the look of holiness.

DEDICATE THE TEMPLE

The Old Testament adds wonderful richness to our faith. From the earliest writings we read of the creation of the heavens and the earth. We gain great confidence as we see God use common men and women to accomplish His purpose - even though these common people had many of our same flaws. The Old Testament also provides a clear picture of a chosen people (the nation of Israel) being taught to worship and live with absolute reverence for God.

After the Israelites were led out of Egypt, God gave instructions to Moses for constructing the Tabernacle. The Tabernacle was made of cloth, animal skins, and poles so it could be easily moved. This was to be the central place of worship and where the presence of God would reside.

After several hundred years, the people of Israel settled into the promised land. God gave King David the vision for a permanent Temple which would replace the mobile Tabernacle. David made plans and collected material, but God waited for Solomon to become king before construction began.

It took Solomon seven years to construct the Temple using over 150,000 workers, (2 Chronicles 2:1-2). When the Temple was complete, the dedication began; sacrifices were made to honor and worship God; music was played and songs were sung "to give praise and thanks to the Lord," (2 Chronicles 5:13).

2 Chronicles 5:13-14

"Then the Temple of the Lord was filled with a cloud, and the priests could not perform their service because of the cloud, for the glory of the Lord filled the Temple of God."

One thousand years after the Temple was dedicated, Jesus died on the cross and we entered into a new covenant with a new Temple: "Don't you know that you yourselves are God's Temple and that God's Spirit lives in you?" (1 Corinthians 3:16).

WE are now the Temple of God. The plans have been developed and the construction is complete - the time has now come for dedication. We must honor Him as Lord and set aside our lives as a holy place for worship (Romans 12:1). As our love and worship becomes focused on God, we will no longer perform "our" service. Everything we do will become His because our lives will be filled with the glory of the Lord. It's time for His glory to completely fill our lives; it's time to dedicate the Temple.

RETURN TO GIVE THANKS

One day when Jesus was traveling from the region of Galilee down to Jerusalem, ten men with leprosy approached Him and called out; "Jesus, Master, have pity on us!" (Luke 17:13). Jesus didn't immediate heal the lepers; rather, He gave them a simple instruction: "Go, show yourselves to the priests," (Luke 17:14).

A leper would only present himself to a priest if he believed the leprosy was gone. The priests had the authority to declare a diseased person ceremonially clean and give him permission to return home (Leviticus 14). Therefore, the lepers demonstrated great faith when they followed Jesus' command: "And as they went, they were cleansed," (Luke 17:14). Notice that the lepers had to take action before they were healed; their action of obedience demonstrated their faith.

Though all ten lepers had been cleansed of their terrible disease, only one returned to give thanks: "He threw himself at Jesus' feet and thanked Him," (Luke 17:16).

Luke 17:17

"Jesus asked, 'Were not all ten cleansed? Where are the other nine?'"

I wonder if we really understand the degree to which we have been healed and made clean - and how we continue to be healed every day. "While we were still sinners, Christ died for us," (Romans 5:8). Do we really comprehend how much He loves us, or how much He gave to people so undeserving of His love? "God made us alive with Christ even when we were dead in transgression," (Ephesians 2:5). We were DEAD, and He made us alive with Christ - that's healing!!

And as we continue on our Christian walk, we receive divine healing in countless ways - but they are healings we most often fail to even recognize. Every time relationships are restored, His hand has healed; when conflicts are resolved, His hand has healed; and when He lovingly welcomes us back after we have wandered from His presence, His hand has healed.

But do we return to thank Him? Or are we as the other nine lepers who go on our way and forget the One to whom we owe our very lives.

The one leper who returned, threw himself at Jesus' feet. If we knew how deathly ill we are without Christ and how completely He has healed our soul, we would not only throw ourselves at His feet, but we would remain and refuse to ever leave. Let's live each day in the presence of God; let's come before Him with hearts overflowing with continual thanksgiving and praise. Let's ALWAYS be the one who will return to give thanks.

TOOLS OF THE TEACHER

In the days of the prophet Jeremiah, God's chosen people had turned away to worship other gods; but God desired for His people to return and longed for them to worship Him as the One True God. The people of Israel had been warned for many years and now God used a foreign king as His tool for discipline and instruction.

Jeremiah 27:6

"Now I will hand all your countries over to my servant Nebuchadnezzar king of Babylon; I will make even the wild animals subject to him."

God reminded the people that He was in control. He also revealed their sinful pride as He required them to submit in order to survive: "Bow your neck under the yoke of the king of Babylon and you will live," (Jeremiah 27:12). Many of the people chose to die rather than trust God's instructions.

There was no indication that Nebuchadnezzar even acknowledged God at this point in his life - and yet, God called him "My servant." It was God's plan to use this non-believing foreigner as a tool to teach His children some very important (and painful) lessons.

Being adopted into God's family through the gift of Salvation is a one time event. Through faith in the sacrifice of Jesus for the forgiveness of our sins, we receive His grace and become "a new creation," (2 Corinthians 5:17). However, learning to "live for God" is an on-going process which will last all the rest of our days.

There is so much our Heavenly Father desires for us to understand - so many lessons He wants us to learn - and yet, all the lessons seem nearly identical. He desires a continual and intimate fellowship; He wants us to learn to trust Him and love Him with all our heart, soul, mind, and strength (Mark 12:30).

As we open our life to God's teaching, we must allow Him to instruct us using the tools of His choice. His lessons are often taught using the most unlikely messengers and through the worst of circumstances; but His lessons always contain a lasting sweetness when they are properly learned.

No matter what we face today, let's look for the lesson God is teaching. We may not appreciate the tools He uses for shaping and molding, but all His instruction is given because He loves us and desires for us to live in His presence and love Him even more. Let's praise Him for His instruction and be thankful for ALL the tools of The Teacher.

AT THE LORD'S COMMAND

When God led Moses and the people of Israel out of Egypt, He had many lessons for them to learn. While on the journey to the promised land, God taught His chosen people about living a life of worship and holiness - but He especially taught about the need for obedience and trust.

Though we often refer to Israel's forty years in the desert as a time of wandering, their movement was very carefully controlled. God gave directions through a cloud which settled over the tabernacle. The cloud appeared as a normal cloud during the day, and at night "the cloud looked like fire," (Numbers 9:15). The movement of the people was directed by the movement of the cloud.

Numbers 9:22-23

"Whether the cloud stayed over the tabernacle for two days or a month or a year, the Israelites would remain in camp and not set out; but when it lifted, they would set out. At the Lord's command they encamped and at the Lord's command they set out."

For forty years, God taught an entire generation the importance of looking to Him for their daily direction. When they set up camp, they didn't know how long they would stay - and when they began to move, they didn't know where they were going or how long they would travel. The importance of the journey was in the lessons of obedience and trust - not in the actual steps along the way.

Today, we are also on a journey to the promised land and God still has many things for us to learn - lessons of worship, holiness, trust, and obedience. We may not have the benefit of a cloud, but if we listen very carefully, we can still "hear" His direction. The same God who directed the Israelites is directing us today - and He longs for us to trust Him and obediently follow.

One of our hardest lessons is to understand that God does not need us to move, nor does He need us to stay. God will accomplish ALL He desires with or without our assistance. But He invites us to join Him and witness the awesome movement of His hand - He invites us to follow.

Our Father is able to direct our steps much better than we can direct them ourself (another difficult lesson). We must learn to listen for His leading by drawing near and living in His presence. Then, whether He says to stay or go, we must trust Him with all our heart and obediently move at the Lord's command.

SECURE IN HIS PRESENCE

Jehoiakim was king of Judah just prior to the first invasion by the Babylonians in 605 B.C. He had become very comfortable in the security of the palace - and an alliance with the Egyptians made him feel even more protected from enemy attacks. With his every need and desire fulfilled - and with all his fears removed - Jehoiakim did not see a reason to listen as God warned him to repent.

Jeremiah 22:18,21

"Therefore this is what the Lord says about Jehoiakim son of Josiah king of Judah... 'I warned you when you felt secure, but you said, 'I will not listen!'""

We seem to spend the majority of our lives building various forms of security. We strive for security in our job, our finances, and our relationships; but we must guard against anything which takes away from our complete dependence on our Heavenly Father. We should be thankful for every one of our blessings, but we must never become so comfortable that we close our eyes and ears to His leading.

Our daily walk is made one slow step at a time, as we "trust in the Lord with all your heart and lean not on your own understanding," (Proverbs 3:5). Usually, we are allowed to see only the next few steps of our journey. God then gives further direction as we step out in faith with what He has already revealed. We may not always know where our path will lead, but we are called to have faith in the One who is leading: "Your Word is a lamp unto my feet," (Psalm 119:105).

We must also be cautious in the way we strive for security in our relationship with God. Activities such as church attendance, Bible study, or various ministries must never define our intimacy with God. Our relationship with Him must be based on faith in Jesus Christ and a pure love which flows from of the innermost part of our heart. All of our activities mean nothing if they fail to lead us into the presence of God.

Let's not allow our lives to develop a sense of security which shuts out the need for God and the hunger to abide in His presence. A walk of faith will always require stepping into the unknown; trust will always require a release of some independence; and true love for God will always require abandoning that which keeps us from Him. Let's lean on Him, love Him, and draw ever closer - let's obtain our security only by being secure in His presence.

MISPLACED TRUST

In the message "Secure In His Presence" we were encouraged to guard against anything which takes away from our complete dependence on our Heavenly Father. We saw how worldly security can sometimes cause us to close our eyes and ears to God's leading. Becoming secure in the world is to also place our trust in the things of the world. King David made this mistake and it cost him dearly.

God described David as "a man after My own heart," (Acts 13:22). David clearly saw God working in his life when he fought Goliath and when he was anointed King of Israel. God protected David through his trials with Saul and led him through many military victories. But toward the end of his reign, David began to trust the world's definition of power and might.

1 Chronicles 21:1-2

"Satan rose up against Israel and incited David to take a census of Israel. So David said to Joab and the commanders of the troops, 'Go and count the Israelites. Then report back to me so that I may know how many there are.'"

God allowed Satan to tempt David because there was deep pride in David that needed to be revealed. There was nothing inherently wrong with counting the people - after all, when God led the nation of Israel out of Egypt, He told Moses: "Take a census of the whole Israelite community," (Numbers 1:2). But David had become very "self" reliant and had placed his trust in his own strength and abilities - and in his available resources.

David recognized his wrong and confessed his sin: "I have sinned greatly by doing this. Now, I beg You, take away the guilt," (1 Chronicles 21:8). Though David's sin was forgiven, God still enforced severe consequences: "So the Lord sent a plague on Israel, and seventy thousand men of Israel fell dead," (1 Chronicles 21:14). As the leader of God's chosen people, David was expected to set an example of complete trust.

God wants and expects the total devotion of our heart - this means all of our love as well as our trust. He establishes our path and grants us the strength to achieve victory on our journey. Let's give Him ALL the glory and honor in everything we do. Let's keep our eyes forever focused on Christ and guard against the sin of misplaced trust.

WHERE ARE YOU

The devil deceived Eve and caused her to disobey God's command. The deception began by first causing Eve to doubt what God said and continued by saying God had not been truthful.

Eve justified her disobedience as being in her best interest, ate the fruit from the forbidden tree, and gave some to her willing husband. As soon as they ate the fruit, they became aware that they were naked and covered themselves with leaves.

Genesis 3:8-9

"Then the man and his wife heard the sound of the Lord God as He was walking in the garden in the cool of the day, and they hid from the Lord God among the trees of the garden. But the Lord God called to the man, 'Where are you?'"

"Where are you?" is an interesting choice of words for the all-knowing Creator of the Universe. God knew exactly where Adam was hiding. He wasn't searching through the bushes trying to find His lost creation: "Aaaaaadaaaaammm....Where aarrrrrree yoouuuuuuu?" No, God was speaking directly to Adam: "Adam, where are you; why are you here? Why are you in this condition? Do you even know where you are or how you got here?"

Adam's willful disobedience caused him to tremble as he answered: "I was afraid because I was naked; so I hid," (Genesis 3:10). Adam was lost. Somehow, even in the paradise of the garden, Adam and Eve had wandered in their relationship with God. They were alone when the deceptions of the devil took hold - and now their sin caused them to hide from God.

ALL sin has its beginning in a separation from God - in a wandering from His presence. We cannot sin if we remain in His presence; if we truly live out our life "in Christ," the conviction of the Spirit is so great that we are not able to walk down the path of temptation that leads to sin.

Do we know where we are? The Apostle Paul tells us to "examine yourselves," (2 Corinthians 13:5). A life outside of God's presence will begin to believe the lie and become susceptible to temptation. A life immersed in sin will desire to run and hide, and will no longer even seek the presence of God.

Let's return to a life of worship where Jesus is the focus of everything we do, say, and think. Let's honestly examine our life and evaluate our closeness with God. Let's make sure we're abiding in His presence when God asks: "Where are you?"

THE EXAMINED LIFE

We've heard it said and it proves to be true; the unexamined life is not worth living. If we flow through life without evaluating who we are and what we believe, we have not really lived. We may give the outward appearance of satisfaction - we may even fool ourselves for a number of years - but until we look deep inside and deal with what we find, there will always be an emptiness.

God knows every detail of our heart: "Nothing in all creation is hidden from God's sight. Everything is uncovered and laid bare before the eyes of Him to whom we must give account," (Hebrews 4:13). But our Heavenly Father desires for us to know ourselves as we are "conformed to the likeness of His Son," (Romans 8:29).

As we seek to understand our heart - with all our hidden motives, pride, and selfishness - we find we're somewhat difficult to understand. Without the Spiritual help which God freely gives, there will be parts of our life which remain covered and dark.

Psalm 139:23-24

"Search me, O God, and know my heart; test me and know my anxious thoughts. See if there is any offensive way in me, and lead me in the way everlasting."

We have been given God's Word as a guide: "a lamp to my feet," (Psalm 119:105). And as we dig deeper into His Word, we find the same lamp which guides our steps also reveals our heart: "The lamp of the Lord searches the spirit of a man; it searches out his inmost being," (Proverbs 20:27).

Using God's Word to truly examine our heart can be painful. It seems we strip back one layer only to expose additional layers we didn't even know we had; "Forgive my hidden faults," (Psalm 19:12). But failure to examine each layer can lead to a hardened heart and a calloused approach toward sin. More importantly, failure to examine what we believe can lead to a life without the Salvation offered only through faith in Jesus.

If we desire an eternity in His presence; if we desire to bring Him the maximum glory and honor which our lives can produce, we must determine today to know ourselves - to know our strengths, our weaknesses, our beliefs, and our desire to follow where He leads. We must be prepared to be searched and washed by His Word. We must be committed to living the examined life.

THE MOST HOLY PLACE

God created Adam and placed him in the Garden of Eden. While in the garden, Adam enjoyed God's presence. God brought Adam the animals to name (Genesis 2:19) and actually walked with Adam during the day. However, this fellowship was broken and man was cast out of God's presence when Adam sinned and ate of the forbidden fruit.

After God called Moses to lead the Israelites out of Egypt, He told Moses to construct a holy place for His presence to reside. God called this the Most Holy Place and instructed that it be separated from the rest of the tabernacle by a curtain.

Leviticus 16:2

"The Lord said to Moses: 'Tell your brother Aaron not to come whenever he chooses into the Most Holy Place behind the curtain in front of the atonement cover on the ark, or else he will die, because I appear in the cloud over the atonement cover.'"

The Most Holy Place could only be entered by the High Priest (a Levite from the line of Aaron), and only once a year on the Day of Atonement. The High Priest would enter the Most Holy Place with the blood of a goat as a sacrifice for the sins of the people, (Leviticus 16:15).

God loved us so much that He gave His Son to be the final sacrifice for our sins: "He did not enter by means of the blood of goats and calves; but He entered the Most Holy Place once for all by his own blood, having obtained eternal redemption," (Hebrews 9:12).

When Jesus died on the cross, "the curtain of the temple was torn in two from top to bottom," (Matthew 27:51). His sacrifice provides a way for us to enter into the presence of God at any moment: "We have confidence to enter the Most Holy Place by the blood of Jesus," (Hebrews 10:19).

Before God created the heavens and the earth - before He set the stars in the sky, drew the boundaries of the sea or formed man from the dust of the ground - He had a plan which would allow us to walk in His presence for all eternity. Before time began, His plan was the sacrifice of Jesus.

God is calling us to reach out and draw near to Him. He is calling us into His presence through faith in the sacrifice of His Son. The Creator of the Universe is knocking at the door: "If anyone hears My voice and opens the door, I will come in and eat with him, and he with Me," (Revelation 3:20). Let's open the door and enter into His presence today - let's enter, and remain, in the Most Holy Place.

SERVE IN OBEDIENCE

David was crowned king over the tribe of Judah soon after Saul died in about the year 1010 BC. About seven years later, all of Israel acknowledged David as their new king.

One of David's first actions as king was to attempt to move the Ark of God from the home of Abinadab to Jerusalem. David and all the officials believed that by making the Ark a more central focus for the nation, God would bless all of Israel.

This was a very exciting time. The Ark was being transported on a new cart pulled by oxen, and over thirty thousand people were "celebrating with all their might before the Lord, with songs and with harps, lyres, tambourines, sistrums and cymbals," (2 Samuel 6:5). But even during this great time of excitement, God demonstrated the necessity of obedience.

2 Samuel 6:6-7

"When they came to the threshing floor of Nacon, Uzzah reached out and took hold of the Ark of God, because the oxen stumbled. The Lord's anger burned against Uzzah because of his irreverent act; therefore God struck him down and he died there beside the Ark of God."

Uzzah's intentions were good - he desired to serve by keeping the Ark from falling to the ground. But these enthusiastic and well intended actions were not directed by God. In fact, they were in conflict with His Word.

God had given instructions that the Ark should be moved with poles (Exodus 25:14-15) and that anyone who touched the Ark must be put to death (Numbers 4:15). Uzzah served where he "thought" there was a need - but he served at the expense of true obedience.

We must ALWAYS be sensitive to God's leading. Seemingly godly action, if done outside the will of God, is sin. We must never assume that what "looks" good and godly is truly of God. His perfect will can only be determined as we enter His presence, worship at His feet, and commune with Him in prayer. Let's continue to serve with great enthusiasm in all we do - but let's remember to always serve in obedience!

REQUEST A PROSPEROUS LIFE

In the middle of a very long list of genealogies, there are a few short verses about a man named Jabez who was a descendant of Judah. We never read about him again, but it appears Jabez was included because of his bold request to God...and because of God's response.

1 Chronicles 4:10

"Jabez cried out to the God of Israel, 'Oh, that You would bless me and enlarge my territory! Let Your hand be with me, and keep me from harm so that I will be free from pain.' And God granted his request."

Sometimes passages on asking and receiving can be difficult to teach. "How much more will your Father in heaven give good gifts to those who ask Him!" (Matthew 7:11). These passages are full of truth, but those who preach the popular prosperity gospel have abused them to say God wants everyone to be financially rich and all we must do is ask; if we can name it, we can claim it - but this is far from the truth.

God DOES want us to prosper: "'For I know the plans I have for you,' declares the Lord, 'plans to prosper you and not to harm you, plans to give you hope and a future,'" (Jeremiah 29:11). And, He DOES want us to ask: "You do not have, because you do not ask God. When you ask, you do not receive, because you ask with wrong motives," (James 4:2-3). God has a plan to prosper us, but it is possible we do not prosper simply because we do not ask with the correct motive.

Before we can properly understand these passages, we must first understand God's definition of prosperity. A Godly prosperity has very little to do with finances or possessions - and a great deal to do with peace and contentment. A prosperous life is also one which bears much fruit - one that completes the work God has asked us to accomplish.

A prosperous life begins by drawing near (and remaining near) to the presence of God. Without first abiding in His presence, we won't even know what to ask for - we won't know what will allow us to "prosper." "Delight yourself in the Lord and He will give you the desire of your heart," (Psalm 37:4). As we draw near to God, He places the desires on our heart which will lead us to true prosperity - then we must ask. It is in the asking and in the expectation of the answer that we exercise our faith and prove it to be real.

Let's ask God to increase our territory - to increase our realm of influence in His Kingdom. Let's ask Him to protect us from harm and to accomplish great things in, and through, all the things we do and say. Let's draw near to God and boldly request a prosperous life.

NEVER TRADE THE BLESSING

When Isaac was sixty years old, his wife Rebecca gave birth to twin sons. Esau was born first, followed immediately by Jacob: "with his hand grasping Esau's heal." (Genesis 25:26). Esau grew up to be a skillful hunter while Jacob stayed more around the tents with his mother.

In the days of Esau and Jacob, the firstborn son was given a special honor called the birthright. The child having the birthright received a double portion of the family inheritance as well as the eventual privilege of family leadership. The birthright could be traded, but all future birthright blessings were then lost.

Genesis 25:29-32

"Once when Jacob was cooking some stew, Esau came in from the open country, famished. He said to Jacob, 'Quick, let me have some of that red stew! I'm famished!' Jacob replied, 'First sell me your birthright.' 'Look, I am about to die,' Esau said. 'What good is the birthright to me?'"

Esau was a young man who lived "in the moment" and traded his birthright for a bowl of stew; he placed much greater value on immediate gratification than on future blessings. In his mind, Esau exaggerated his immediate need in order to justify the future loss. The mighty hunter may have been hungry - maybe even VERY hungry - but he certainly was not about to die.

We see similar trades being made today. When a child leaves home in rebellion, they trade an honoring relationship with their parents for the perceived pleasures of immediate freedom. When a spouse pursues a relationship outside on marriage, they have traded a God-honoring union for the perceived pleasures of the flesh.

When we fail to "wait upon the Lord," and instead, make hasty decisions with a job, a move, a relationship, or a major purchase, we have traded the blessing of God's perfect will.

What bowl of stew are we trading for today? God has promised a blessing for those who believe in Jesus - those who trust in Him for the forgiveness of sin and walk daily in His light. He has promised to set us free to live a life of true peace, purpose, and contentment - and an eternal glory when we die. ALL worldly pleasures will fade away: "For what is seen is temporary, but what is unseen is eternal," (2 Corinthians 4:18). Let's live each day in the presence of God and give Him every part of our life in pure and holy worship - let's love Him with all our heart and never trade the blessing.

A TASTE OF ETERNITY

In our Christian walk, we must learn to maintain an eternal perspective where we consider our life on an eternal time scale and weigh our current burdens against the eternal glory of Heaven. Unfortunately, many believers are unable to gain strength or comfort from this view of life. Although they know the concept, they lack anything on which to base their hope.

This is unfortunate, but understandable. If our view of Heaven contains no real foundation, how can the thought of eternity make our troubles seem "light and momentary?" (2 Corinthians 4:17). And while it's true that "faith is the substance of things hoped for," (Hebrews 11:1), we still need some understanding of what we hope, or our faith will not truly impact our life.

When Jacob was looking for a wife, he found Rachel. Jacob quickly fell in love and promised to work seven years in exchange for receiving Rachel as his wife.

Genesis 29:20

"So Jacob served seven years to get Rachel, but they seemed like only a few days to him because of his love for her."

Jacob worked hard for many years, but the hope of being with the one he loved eased any burden he might have felt. Jacob saw Rachel's beauty every day. He probably spent many hours dreaming of her and of holding her in his arms. There was undoubtedly a longing inside Jacob which he knew only Rachel could fill. Jacob had a clear understanding of his hope - and it brought him great comfort.

God gave His Son so we could be brought back to a full and right relationship with Him for all eternity. But God did not leave us with an empty view or ask us to cling to a blind hope. He allows us into His presence and gives us the ability to know Him - NOW! We will never grasp all that Heaven has to offer until we see Him face to face. But God allows us to taste eternity if we will only draw near and ask.

Let's dedicate our lives to knowing the One with whom we will spend eternity - the One on whom we base our hope. Let's commune with our Father in prayer and learn of His nature through His Word. Let's strive for an all-consuming love - a love complete with the empty ache which only His presence can fill. Let's rejoice, receive comfort and gain strength, as we draw near and are allowed a taste of eternity.

THE CHALLENGE TO DRAW NEAR

The letters of the Apostle Paul comprise much of the New Testament. His letters were written to give instruction on the Christian faith and to encourage perseverance through times of testing. Paul often wrote of the simplicity of the gospel message: "For it is by grace you have been saved, through faith - and this not from yourselves, it is the gift of God.," (Ephesians 2:8). But he also wrote to encourage those who put their faith in Jesus to live a life of service, holiness, and unity.

When we accept Jesus Christ as our Lord and Savior, we begin a new life. We are set free from the bondage of sin (Romans 6:22), and are called to follow Christ as we are conformed to His image (Romans 8:29). But Paul saw many believers, sitting on the sidelines of the Christian life, in desperate need of encouragement.

Ephesians 4:1

"As a prisoner for the Lord, then, I urge you to live a life worthy of the calling you have received."

Paul gives encouragement by "urging" a worthy life. The word used for urge can also be translated as beseech, beg, implore, exhort, or challenge. This is not a pat on the back which says, "You're doing well, keep running a good race!" - this is a challenging plea to draw nearer to God and give our lives more fully to Him.

Romans 12:1

"Therefore, I urge {beg, implore, exhort, and even challenge} you, brothers, in view of God's mercy, to offer your bodies as living sacrifices, holy and pleasing to God - this is your Spiritual act of worship."

Today, we are being challenged! We are challenged to trust God more - to talk to Him more and seek His presence more diligently! We are challenged to walk firmly on His path and not get pulled away by the lies of the world! We are challenged to love our Heavenly Father with all our heart, soul, mind and strength (Mark 12:30). As we face this day with its multitude of struggles, let's live a life worthy of the calling we have received and answer the challenge to draw near!

A GOD OF CONVENIENCE

Paul had been arrested and sent to Caesarea to stand trial before Governor Felix. During Paul's trial, he spoke of his worship of God and belief in His Word. Felix kept Paul in prison, but often talked with him about his faith.

Acts 24:24-25

"He sent for Paul and listened to him as he spoke about faith in Christ Jesus. As Paul discoursed on righteousness, self-control and the judgment to come, Felix was afraid and said, 'That's enough for now! You may leave. When I find it convenient, I will send for you.'"

Governor Felix had the ability to hear the gospel from the greatest theologian of all time (other than Jesus Himself), and yet failed to act on what he heard.

During Jesus' ministry, Herod had arrested John the Baptist for speaking against his marriage (Herod was married to his brother's wife). Though Herod wanted to kill John, he also feared and respected him because he was a righteous and holy man; "When Herod heard John, he was greatly puzzled; yet he liked to listen to him," (Mark 6:20). Herod liked to listen to John's uncompromising message of repentance, and yet he failed to act on what he heard.

Pilate came face to face with the Son of God. He heard Jesus calmly claim to be King of the Jews and to have special favor from God; "You would have no power over Me if it were not given to you from above," (John 19:11). Pilate listened to Jesus, found no fault, and tried to set Him free (John 19:12) - but in the end, Pilate failed to act on the truth, he failed to act on what he heard.

Most of us experience a wonderful religious freedom today. We have free access to God's Word and can usually find a local church willing to preach the truth. Yet, how often do we fail to act? How often do our religious activities become cold and mechanical, lacking any real interest? "These people come near to Me with their mouth and honor Me with their lips, but their hearts are far from Me," (Isaiah 29:13).

If our worship does not invade every area of our life, then God is not on the throne. We must trust Him in ALL things! We must have a passion for His Word as well as an uncompromising willingness to act. We must long for His presence each and every day - not just during our once a week worship.

Let's NEVER put God on the shelf or ask Him to just be "available" in case of an emergency. He's the Creator of the Universe who has called us to a life of full time worship. Let's never treat our Heavenly Father as a God of convenience.

WORSHIP FROM THE HEART

In the message "A God of Convenience" we were encouraged to be true worshipers who walked with God every day and refused to put Him "on the shelf." We must never become people who go through the motions of worshiping with our lips, but have hearts that are far from God, (Isaiah 29:13). We must be careful not to stray from the path of devoted love and become entangled in the vines of selfish convenience.

But how can we guard against such wandering - how can we recognize when we are beginning to stray?

Passion! Our relationship with God is not based on an exercise of the intellect - it is based on a transformation of the heart. Our relationship began with a work of the Spirit as our heart became His. It must now continue with a renewed passion where we are walking so close that our only desire is to give Him ALL our heart.

David's Kingdom was in total rebellion. His son, Absalom, was attempting to become the new king and had forced David to flee into the desert. With his life's work falling apart and far from his home and place of worship, David turned to God and gave us a clear picture of Godly passion.

Psalm 63:1-4

"O God, You are my God, earnestly I seek You; my soul thirsts for You, my body longs for You, in a dry and weary land where there is no water. I have seen You in the sanctuary and beheld Your power and Your glory. Because Your love is better than life, my lips will glorify You. I will praise You as long as I live, and in Your name I will lift up my hands."

Although it may be difficult to maintain this level of passion every moment of the day, this IS the relationship to which we have been called. This is worship. We must realize that this world is a "dry and weary land" when compared to walking in His presence. We must long for God's love more than life itself.

If this type of relationship sounds foreign - maybe even a little radical - then I invite you to "taste and see that the Lord is good," (Psalm 34:8). He will pour out His blessings if you will step out in faith and draw near. If you understand this relationship but realize the passion has faded, then I exhort you to return. Return to what you know will truly satisfy - to what you know is eternal. Let's all step closer and passionately worship from the heart.

'

IN WHOM WE TRUST

Hezekiah became King of Judah soon after the northern tribes of Israel had been taken captive by the Assyrians. Judah was now being threatened by this same enemy. Hezekiah was young and had a strong desire to do right in the eyes of God - but his faith was being tested.

Seeing that his kingdom would soon be under attack from the mighty Assyrians, Hezekiah sought help through an alliance with the Egyptians. Though this alliance was not wrong in itself, the action was taken out of fear and without consulting God. Therefore, the alliance was a sin! The prophet Isaiah made this clear with strong, but wise, counsel.

Isaiah 31:1

"Woe to those who go down to Egypt for help, who rely on horses, who trust in the multitude of their chariots and in the great strength of their horsemen, but do not look to the Holy One of Israel, or seek help from the Lord."

Hezekiah made the same mistake which is all too common among believers today. We say we believe God's Word is true, but we fail to trust Him in the real trials of life. It was much easier for Hezekiah to place his trust in the Egyptian horses and chariots, which he understood and could see, than in the Almighty Hand of God which he "believed," but which remained unseen.

By the time the Assyrian's attacked, Hezekiah's faith had greatly increased. As he spoke with his soldiers, Hezekiah demonstrated his full confidence in God.

2 Chronicles 32:7-8

"Do not be afraid or discouraged because of the king of Assyria and the vast army with him, for there is a greater power with us than with him. With him is only the arm of flesh, but with us is the Lord our God to help us and to fight our battles."

When the enemy attacks, where do we run? If our faith is restricted to the inside of church walls on Sunday morning, we will definitely be ill-prepared for battle. We must learn to walk in the presence of God and converse with Him - worship Him - all through our day.

When we trust Him and love Him with ALL our heart, we begin to walk in victory regardless of the physical outcome of a particular battle. With our eyes firmly set on Jesus, the war has already been won. When we are under attack, let's put substance to our faith and allow our lives to demonstrate in Whom we trust!

ENTER HIS SANCTUARY

In Psalm 73, the writer shows frustration at the things he sees in the world. He can't understand how the wicked can be so carefree and yet so successful. "For I envied the arrogant when I saw the prosperity of the wicked," (Psalm 73:3). He felt he may have wasted his time maintaining Godly values. "Surely in vain have I kept my heart pure; in vain have I washed my hands in innocence," (Psalm 73:13).

He kept searching for answers, but none were found until he began to worship in the presence of God.

Psalm 73:16-17

"When I tried to understand all this, it was oppressive to me - till I entered the sanctuary of God; then I understood."

Many issues in life simply cannot be resolved through our human understanding and reasoning. We try to make sense of our situation and search for the proper solution, but we're often left just shaking our head. During these times of frustration, we need to remember we're a child of God - children of the Creator of the Universe!

Our Heavenly Father does not function according to a set of human rules. And His workings will most often not be understood by human reasoning: "As the heavens are higher than the earth, so are My ways higher than your ways," (Isaiah 55:9). To understand the ways of God, we must be prepared to leave our reason behind and worship Him with our complete trust; "The fear {reverence} of the Lord is the beginning of knowledge," (Proverbs 1:7).

When we are able to worship in His sanctuary - "whether well fed or hungry, whether living in plenty or in want," (Philippians 4:12) - we will begin to see through the eyes of God. The pieces of our life which seem painfully confusing and disconnected will become clear as we see how they fit neatly into God's perfect plan.

Psalm 73:25

"Whom have I in Heaven but You?   And earth has nothing I desire besides You."

Let's return to the place where He's everything we desire and all we really need; in the context of eternity, He's all we really have! Let's worship Him with all our heart and begin to understand as we enter His sanctuary!

LIVING IN HIS PRESENCE

The devotions in this book have focused on our desire and our need to be in the presence of God. Even though we may be terribly entangled with the concerns of the world, every child of God is called and inwardly drawn to His presence.

It should come as no surprise that God's presence does not reside in a building. He does not just "show up" when we gather and sing songs. He doesn't "appear" simply because we jump up and down.

Matthew 28:20
"And surely I am with you always, to the very end of the age."

The presence of God is with us - right now! One of the great blessings most believers miss is being in His presence each and every day. This is very sad because He is much closer than we think, desires our communion much more than we realize, and, as we continue to live in His presence, will pour out His blessings with a much greater abundance than we can imagine.

We need only open our heart to the leading of His Spirit and enter into His presence. We do this by continually "conversing" with God throughout the day and presenting EVERY thought, word, and deed at His feet as our best offering of love. All we do should be done out of love for our Heavenly Father and for the purpose of bringing Him glory.

As unrealistic as this may sound, this is the worship God desires - and the worship He deserves.

Given the choice, would we choose to walk in His presence today? If so, then we must begin! At first, this practice will require great discipline. Our thoughts will stray and we will often step away from His presence. When this happens, we must not become discouraged - we must simply step back in, love Him with all our heart, and continue. As we abide more and more in His presence, we will know Him better, love Him more, and remain with greater ease.

His presence is available to every believer! Some jobs or home environments may pose a greater challenge than others, but He has promised to be with those who desire to walk with Him - regardless of the circumstances. Let's determine today, once and for all, to bring Him glory and honor in ALL we do, say, and think. Let's determine to spend the rest of our days living in His presence.